Here's To
GOOD FOOD

Cooking with Beer, Wine, Liquor and Liqueurs

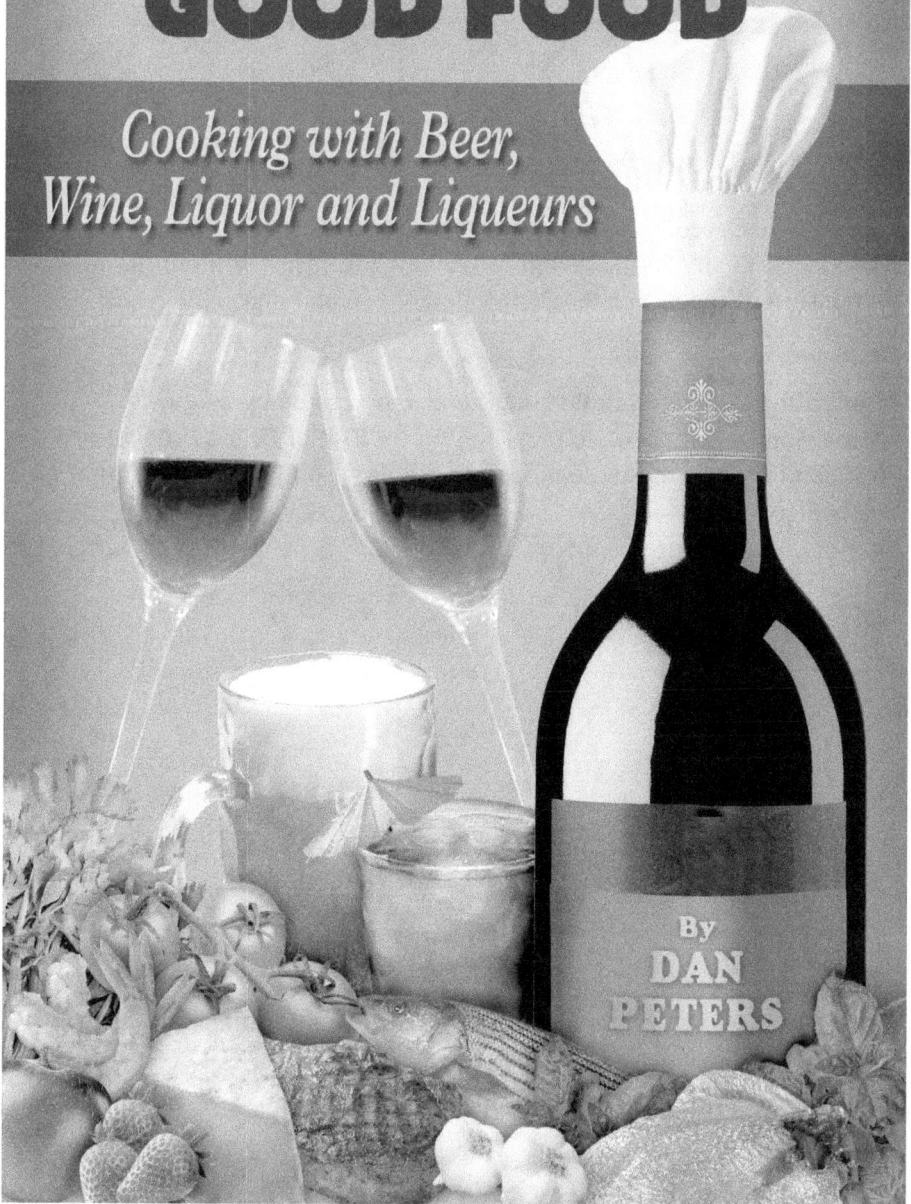

By
DAN
PETERS

HERE'S TO GOOD FOOD
Cooking with Beer, Wine, Liquor and Liqueurs

Copyright 2008 Daniel Peters Production LLC

Published by

Daniel Peters Productions LLC

PO Box 691 Somerville NJ 08876

www.danielpeters.net

ISBN #978-0-615-20936-4

Manufactured in the United States of America

ACKNOWLEDGEMENTS

Graphic Designer
Kathy Moncelsi

Editorial Assistant
Elizabeth Turner

Thanks to Max, Sharon, Ed, Margo, Kathy, Dolores, Tunde, Cecilia, Queen Ally, Jersey Adobe Multimedia and all other contributors.

Extra special thanks to Sister Carol Ann
and dear family and friends.

CONTENTS

Quiz answers can be found at the end of each chapter.

INTRODUCTION

Food is often the centermost attraction when people gather for good cheer. Breathing life into a party can be effected simply by injecting vibrancy into the gathering's fare.

On a day to day basis, mundane menus all too often creep into prevalence. An interminable cycle of meat loaf and canned peas can provoke one's palate to scream for the piquant.

Whether preparing food for one or one hundred, seasoning with alcohol imparts a flavoring of intrigue unattainable with any other ingredients. Indeed, beyond providing a short cut to flair, the blending of food and spirits can be more like conjuring than cooking.

Something transcendental occurs the very moment that a potent potable instills its magic in food.

Witness how adding wine to a dish creates elegance in an instant. In a flash whiskey brings invigoration to any cuisine it encounters, and food suddenly becomes fun with the infusion of a brew.

Presto! Tequila causes a culinary transformation, while an imported liqueur immediately adds exoticism.

Fiery. Zesty. Sophisticated. Charming. The many nuances of alcohol in cooking enable any intrepid preparer to light up a lunch or raise a dinner to new heights with a modicum of effort.

Teetotalers can take heart in the knowledge that in many recipes the alcohol dissipates in the cooking process, leaving only a richly enhanced flavor in your meticulously prepared creation.

On the other hand, if a ringing timer interrupts you in the middle of a nip, pause and remember that the point is after all to savor the joys of indulgence.

A happy cook is a good cook.

Here's to good food.

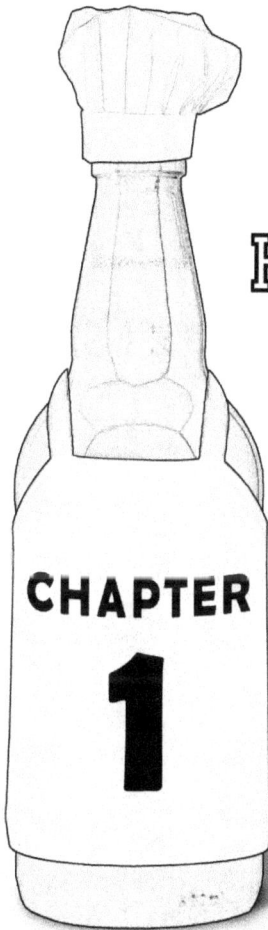

HERE'S TO COOKING WITH BEER

CHAPTER 1

Cooking with BEER has long been an art practiced by the world's most celebrated cooks who often use beer as the secret ingredient in their most delicious recipes. And no wonder - for beer provides a savory flavor and light texture to many, many foods.

This sparkling, effervescent and refreshing beverage can be ideally married to anything from a gourmet meal to convenience food.

1

MARGO'S CHEESY BEER DIP

1/4 CUP BEER
8 oz. Softened Cheddar Cheese
8 oz. Cream Cheese
2 Cloves of Garlic

Pinch Crushed Parsley
Dash of Paprika
Splash of Worchester or Hot Sauce
1 tsp. Dried Dill

Soften cream cheese in microwave, mix with cheddar cheese.

Combine all ingredients by whipping with whisk until creamy.

Refrigerate 1 to 2 hours minimum. Keep cold until ready to serve.

QUICK SWISS FONDUE

1/4 CUP BEER
4 oz. Swiss Cheese

4 oz. Sharp Cheddar Cheese
French Bread

20 minutes before serving, place a 2 quart fondue pot on stand over medium heat, add 1/4 CUP BEER and cook until hot but not boiling.

With spoon, gradually stir in 4 oz. Swiss Cheese chopped and one 4 oz. pkg. of Sharp Cheddar Cheese. Stir until cheese is melted and mixture is smooth. Reduce heat to low. Serve with chunks of French Bread.

PRINCETON RAREBIT

1 1/4 CUPS ALE
1/2 Lb. Grated Sharp Cheddar

4 thick slices of White Bread
Spicy Mustard & Butter

Preheat oven to 225 F. Place cheese in baking dish and cover with mustard to taste.

Pour in ale and bake until cheese is melted.

Toast bread and butter one side then sprinkle lightly with ale. Pour the cheese mixture over the bread and serve.
Serves 4.

WELSH RAREBIT

1/2 CUP BEER
1 Lb. aged Cheddar Cheese,
    Grated
1/8 Tsp. Cayenne

1/2 Tsp. Dry Mustard
1 Tsp. Worcestershire Sauce
1 Tsp. Butter
Salt to Taste

In chafing dish or double boiler over hot (not boiling) water, melt butter and cheese.

As cheese begins to melt, gradually stir in beer. Cook only until smooth and hot.

Stir in seasonings and serve immediately on hot crisp toast or heated crackers.

Makes 4 to 6 Servings.

For a GRILLED RAREBIT, pour the smooth sauce into a shallow, heat proof casserole and broil only until the surface is bubbly and lightly browned.

Place the casserole on a large platter and surround it with toast triangles.

Serve with beer and a green salad.

BEER QUIZ QUESTION 1

Where was the first beer brewed?

A) Russia

B) Africa

C) China

D) Bavaria

BEER FRIED ONION RINGS

1 1/2 CUPS BEER   **1 1/4 Cups All Purpose Flour**
4 Large Onions   **Vegetable Oil**

In a bowl, combined flour and beer.

Blend thoroughly and cover bowl. Leave at room temperature at least 3 hours.

Peel onions and slice into 1/4 inch rings.

Heat oil in large frying pan until very hot (not smoking) and dip several onion rings at a time in batter and place in hot oil.

Fry until golden brown.

Place cooked rings on paper towel and keep warm in 200 degree oven.

Serves 4 to 6 people.

BEER SOUP

3 CUPS (2 CANS) BEER   **2 Whole Eggs**
6 Tsp. Sugar   **1 Cup Milk**
1/8 Tsp. Cinnamon   **1/3 Cup Sour Cream**

Place sugar and beer into sauce pan over medium heat. Cook until sugar is melted. Stir occasionally.

In another pan heat milk and cinnamon.
Do not boil.
Put eggs and sour cream in bowl and beat with whisk until smooth.
Add hot beer mixture, beating rapidly with whisk. Add milk and continue to beat.
Pour soup into large sauce pan and heat thoroughly, stirring constantly.
Do not boil.
If soup should curdle slightly, strain.

Yield 4 to 6 servings.

BEANTOWN CLAM CHOWDER

1 CUP BAVARIAN DARK BEER OR OKTOBERFEST
5 Tbsp. Butter
4 Oz. Bacon
4 Medium Onions
1 1/2 Cups Chicken Stock
5 Medium Baking Potatoes, peeled and grated
1 Tsp. Dried Basil
1 1/2 lbs. chopped clams with juice
2 cups milk
Salt and Pepper to taste

In large soup pan heat 2 tablespoons butter over medium heat. Add bacon and saute until slightly crisp.

Remove bacon from pan and set aside.

Add remaining butter and cook onions until wilted.

Remove from pan and set aside.

Pour chicken stock and beer into same pot and cook over medium heat.

Add grated potatoes, basil, bacon and onions and bring to a boil. Simmer for about 1 hour.

Reduce heat and add clams and clam juice and slowly stir in milk.

(For a richer soup, substitute light cream.)

Heat until soup bubbles gently. Add salt and pepper.

Serve in deep soup mugs and garnish with chopped scallions (optional).

STATEN ISLAND STEW

2 1/2 CUPS BROWN ALE
2 Tbsps. Vegetable Oil
1 1/2 lbs. Cubed Stew Meat
5 Large Onions
Salt & Pepper to Taste

1 Tbsp. Brown Sugar
1 Tbsps. Flour
2 Cloves Garlic, crushed
Mustard

In large pot, brown meat on all sides in hot oil.

Chop onions and add to meat and stir until brown.

Lower heat and add brown sugar, garlic and flour. Cook for 4 minutes while stirring constantly.

Add the ale. Season.

Raise heat and bring to boil. Simmer slowly for 2 hours.

About 1/2 hour before serving, remove excess fat and pour stew into casserole dish.

Cut French bread into thick slices and coat with mustard. Place slices on top of casserole and place under grill for about 12 minutes or until bread is brown and crispy.

Serves 4 people.

BLUE CHEESE AND BEER SALAD DRESSING

1/3 CUP BEER
3/4 Cup Mayonnaise
1/2 Cup Sour Cream
1 Tsp. Balsamic Vinegar

1 Small Onion, finely chopped
2 Scallions, finely chopped
1 1/2 Tsp. Hot Sauce

Place mayonnaise and sour cream in bowl.

Stir in onions, vinegar and hot sauce.

Refrigerate before serving.

BEER WAFFLES

1 1/2 PINTS BEER	2 Eggs
2 1/2 Cups Sifted Flour	2 Tblsps. Grated Lemon Rind
1/2 Tsp. Salt	1 Tsp. Fresh Lemon Juice
1/2 Cup Vegetable Oil	1/2 Tsp. Vanilla Extract

Combine all ingredients in deep bowl. Beat until smooth. Let stand at room temperature for 2 hours to rise slightly.

If for breakfast, store unrisen in refrigerator overnight and use without further rising.

Spread small amount of batter on waffle iron. Watch while baking since waffles brown quickly.

Good served with sour cream and brown sugar.

Makes 14 to 16 waffles.

BEER QUIZ QUESTION 2

What gives beer a bitter flavor?

A) Hops

B) Malt

C) Barley

D) Grain

BEER GARDEN OMELET

2 TSP. LIGHT BEER   Salt and Pepper to Taste
2 Tbsp. Butter or Margarine   Hot Sauce or Steak Sauce
2 Eggs

Beat eggs lightly with fork in small bowl.

Add beer, salt and pepper and sauce. Place butter or margarine in omelet pan or 9 inch frying pan. Heat until bubbly.

Do not burn butter.

Pour egg mixture into hot pan and rotate the pan to cover entire bottom with egg mixture. Cook until bottom of omelet is slightly brown.

Put filling on 1/2 of omelet.

Carefully slide omelet out of pan folding in half.

Serve immediately.

SUGGESTED FILLINGS

Sauted mushroom, onions and green pepper slices.

Grated swiss cheese, parmesan cheese and parsley.

Leftover meat such as beef, ham or chicken, strips of green chili and leftover cheese.

Ham, bacon, and grated onion.

Fresh berries (in season).

Sprinkle powdered sugar on omelet.

BE CREATIVE AND USE ANY COMBINATION!

PASSIONATE POTATO PANCAKES

2 CUPS BEER	**2 Eggs**
4 Large Baking Potatoes	**1/2 Cup Italian Bread crumbs**
1 Tsp. Salt	**1 Cup Grated Parmesan Cheese**
1 Cup Olive Oil	**1/4 Tsp. Black Pepper**

Peel and coarsely grate potatoes. Soak in beer for 1 hour. Drain.

(Beer can be saved for another recipe.)

Add eggs, bread crumbs, salt and pepper to potatoes.

Place fry pan over medium heat until hot. Add enough oil to just cover bottom of pan.

Drop several tablespoons of potato mixture into hot oil and flatten slightly. When bottom is golden brown, flip pancake over and brown the other side.

Place in warm oven to keep hot until serving time.

Serves 6.

BRUSSEL SPROUTS IN BEER

4 CANS BEER	**1/2 Tsp. Salt**
3 Boxes Frozen Brussel Sprouts	**2 Tbsps. Butter or Margarine**

Place Brussel Sprouts in large pot and cover with beer. Bring to a boil then reduce heat and simmer for 10 minutes or until tender.

Add salt and butter. Sprouts will absorb beer.

Drain excess.

Serve as a side dish with your favorite meat or fish.

Serves 4.

CARROTS IN BEER

1 CUP BEER	1/2 Tsp. Salt
5 Large Carrots	2 Tbsp. Butter or Margarine
1 Tsp. Sugar	

Peel carrots and slice into thin julienne slices.

In medium fry pan melt butter and add beer and carrots. Bring to boil. Reduce heat and simmer until carrots are tender.

Add Salt and sugar.

Cook for 5 minutes.

Serves 6.

GOODENUFF POTATO SALAD

1/4 CUP BEER	1 Cup Mayonnaise
Six Large Potatoes	3/4 Cup Sour Cream
1/2 Finely Chopped Onions	Salt and Pepper to Taste
1/2 Cup Celery, Diced Small	1/2 lb. Bacon,
	cooked until crisp

Boil potatoes until just tender. Do not overcook.

Peel and cut into thick slices after potatoes have cooled.

Add onions, celery and bacon.

Blend mayonnaise, sour cream and beer thoroughly. Add to potatoes. Season to taste and gently mix salad.

This dish can be served cold or place in 325 oven for 20 minutes for a warm potato salad.

Serves 4 to 6.

YANKEE COLESLAW

1/2 CUP BEER	1/3 Cup Sugar
1 Large Green Cabbage	1 Tsp. Celery Seed
1/4 Head Red Cabbage	1 1/2 Tsp. Mustard
1 Carrot, Grated	Salt and Pepper to Taste
2 Cups Mayonnaise	1 Medium onion, finely chopped

Finely shred cabbage. Add carrots and onion.

In a bowl combine remaining ingredients.

Add dressing to cabbage, season to taste and mix thoroughly.

Chill for several hours.

CALL IT A DAY CASSEROLE

1 1/4 CUPS DARK BEER	3 Carrots, sliced in rounds
2 lbs. Stew Meat	2 lbs. Potatoes, sliced in rounds
3 Large onions, thinly sliced	Salt and Pepper to Taste

Preheat oven to 400 degrees.

Place a layer of meat into bottom of casserole dish. Add a layer of vegetables. Finish with potatoes on top.

Pour beer into casserole until three quarters filled.

Cover and bake for 2 hours then uncover and bake for 30 minutes longer.

Check casserole to make sure it is not too dry.

Add more beer if necessary.

Serves 6.

FLEMISH FLANK STEAK WITH ONION MUSHROOM BEER SAUCE

3/4 CUP LIGHT BEER
1 lb. Flank Steak
1 Tbsps. Worcestershire Sauce
1 Tbsp. Mustard
4 oz. Can Mushrooms,
   undrained

1/4 Tsp. Each:
   Dried Sage
   Thyme
   Pinch ofThyme, Garlic Powder
   1 Small Onion, thinly sliced

Spread meat on both sides with Worcestershire sauce. Spread the top of the meat with mustard.

Spray a large skillet or electric fry pan with cooking spray. Place the meat in the cold skillet, mustard-side up. Raise heat to high.

Cook undisturbed until underside is well browned. Turn meat over and cook to desired doneness (best if very rare).

Remove to a heated platter.

Combine remaining ingredients in skillet. Cook and stir 5 minutes, until most of the liquid has evaporated.

Slice steak thinly against the grain and spoon sauce over steak.

Serves 4.

RUMP ROAST REPAST

1 CAN BEER
7 or 8 lb. Rump Roast
2 Tbsp. Vinegar

2 Tbsp. Parsley
1/2 Tsp. Salt
2 Onions, cut up coarsely

Pour vinegar over roast. Let set at room temperature for 1 hour. Place in roaster and pour beer over roast.

Place onion over meat, add seasoning, cover and bake at 350 degrees for 3 hours.

SAUCY STEAK SAUCE

1 1/2 CUPS DARK BEER
1/2 CUP DRY SHERRY
1/4 Cup Apricot Preserves
1/3 Cup Soy Sauce
1/8 Tsp. Red Pepper Flakes

1/2 Medium Onion
5 Cloves Garlic
1/4 cup Wine Vinegar
1/3 Tsp. Liquid Smoke
1/2 Tsp. Black Pepper

Place all ingredients in heavy duty blender.

Blend on high until smooth.

Put mixture in pot and bring to boil.

Lower heat and simmer for about 15 minutes.

JEWISH MEATBALLS

1 CAN BEER
2 Small Onions
2 Slices White Bread Soaked
  in Water

2 Lbs Chopped Meat
2 Eggs
1 Bottle Ketchup
1 Bottle Chili Sauce

In bowl, mix meat, eggs, onions and crumbled bread.

Form into 2 inch meatballs.

Add small amount of oil in skillet and brown meatballs.

In separate bowl, combine ketchup, chili sauce and beer.

Add to skillet and cook meatballs for 1 hour on low heat.

Makes about 2 dozen meatballs.

BARNIE'S PORK ROAST

1 CUP BEER	1/2 Tsp. Oregano
1 Five Lb. Loin Pork Roast	1/2 Tsp. Coriander
1 Large Onion	2 Carrots, Coarsely Chopped
1 1/2 Tsp. Salt	1 Clove Garlic, Crushed

Place pork in roasting pan. Rub meat with spices. Put onions and carrots around roast and add beer. Roast, covered in 400 degree oven for 2 and 1/2 hours or until pork is no longer pink inside. Do not overcook. Add more beer if bottom of pan begins to dry out. Baste occasionally.

Slice pork and serve with Mexican Sauce.

Serves 6 to 8.

Mexican Sauce: In small pan heat 2 tablespoons olive oil. Add 1 medium onion, chopped finely and 1 chopped clove garlic. Gently saute until slightly brown. Do not overcook, since garlic tends to burn quickly.

Drain 1 large can green tomatoes (Tomatillos), and save liquid.

In electric blender, puree cooked onion and garlic, 1/2 teaspoon cilantro and tomato liquid. Pour puree into sauce pan and bring to boil. Lower heat and simmer for 20 minutes.

Remove from stove and add wine vinegar, salt and pepper.

Serve chilled over pork.

BEER QUIZ QUESTION 3

What is the capacity of a pilsner glass?

A) 6 oz.
B) 8 oz.
C) 10 oz.
D) 12 oz.

BEER AND PORK CHOP CASSEROLE

12 OUNCES BEER
3 Large Sweet Potatoes,
  peeled and sliced
2 Tbsp. Brown Sugar
4 Tbsp. Melted Butter
1 Large Onion, peeled
  and sliced

3 Tart Apples, peeled,
  cored and sliced
2 Tbsp. Flour
1 Tsp. Salt
4 1.5 inch thick pork chops,
  browned

Advance Preparation

Layer sweet potatoes in bottom of greased 3-quart casserole. Sprinkle with sugar and 2 tablespoons butter. Add onion and apples. Top with pork chops. Dissolve flour and salt in remaining butter. Gradually add beer. Pour into casserole, cover and cook in preheated 350 degree oven for 1.5 hours.

Final Preparation

Reheat casserole on stove top. Return to preheated 350 degree oven and bake uncovered for 1.5 hours. Serve directly from pot.
Serves 4.

PAUL'S PORK SKEWERS

1 CUP BEER
1/4 Cup Wine Vinegar
2 Tsp. Dried Parsley
1 Tsp. Dried Basil
2 Tsp. Dried Oregano
1 Tsp. Hot Chili Powder
1 Small Onion, Minced

5 Cloves Garlic
1 Tsp. Black Pepper
4 lbs. Cubed Pork
2 Large Onions, Cut in Chunks
2 lbs. Small Boiled Potatoes
2 Lg. Red Peppers, Cleaned and
  Sliced Thickly

Combine all spices and beer. Marinate pork overnight.

Skewer alternating rows of pork and vegetables and grill until meat is cooked.

SIX-PACK SAMMY'S PORK RIBS

12 OZ. ALE
1/4 Cup Vegetable Oil
1 White Onion, Chopped
6 Lbs. Pork Ribs
1 1/2 Cup Chunky Apple Sauce

4 Chicken Bouillon Cubes
1/4 Cup Wine Vinegar
1/4 Cup Brown Sugar
1 12 Oz. Can Tomato Sauce
1 Tsp. cayenne, black pepper, cumin and coriander

In large saucepan heat ale, bouillon, and vinegar until cubes are dissolved. Add spices and simmer slowly for 15 minutes.

Saute onions in oil until wilted then add garlic and cook only until garlic is slightly brown.

Place onion and garlic mixture into ale. Add applesauce and simmer for 5 minutes.

Cut ribs into portion size and marinate in ale overnight.

(Ribs can be barbecued or grilled on stove.)

Serves 4 to 6.

BEER BOILED KIELBASY

3/4 CUP BEER

1 Lb. Precooked Kielbasy

Place beer in medium pot. Add kielbasy and bring to boil. Reduce heat, cover and simmer for ten minutes.

(If using uncooked kielbasy, increase cooking time to 20 minutes.)

Make sure that beer does not dry up. Add more if necessary.

(This recipe can also be made with bratwurst).

Serves 4.

BEER BARBEQUED SAUSAGE

3 CUPS BEER
3 Pounds Uncooked Sausages, such as Sweet or Hot Italian Sausages,
Bratwurst, Chorizo or Linguica
1 Onion, thinly sliced
About 1 Tablespoon Vegetable Oil
Mustard, for serving

Prick each sausage a half-dozen times with a fork.

Arrange the onion slices on the bottom of a sauté pan just large enough to hold all the sausages. Place the sausages on top and add beer and water to cover (the ratio should be about 3 parts beer to 1 part water).

Place the pan over medium heat and gradually bring the liquid to a simmer, not a rapid boil.

Poach the sausages until half-cooked, 4 to 5 minutes.

Transfer the sausages to a rack on a baking sheet to drain or drain in a colander.

Separate the sausages into links.

Set up the grill for direct grilling and preheat to medium-high.

When ready to cook, brush and oil the grill grate. Lightly brush the sausages on all sides with oil and place on the hot grate.

Grill until the casings are crisp and nicely browned and the sausages are cooked through, 4 to 6 minutes per side.

Should flare-ups arise, move the sausages to a different section of the grill.

Cut lightly into a sausage to test for doneness.

Transfer the sausages to plates or a platter and let rest for 3 minutes.

Serve with plenty of mustard.

Serves 6 to 8

BOWL OF FIRE

3 CUPS BEER	1 Tbsp. Coriander
4 lbs. Stew Meat	10 Cloves Garlic, Mashed
4 lbs. Cubed Pork	1 Tsp. Cayenne Pepper
1 lb. Bacon, Cooked until crisp	1 1/2 Tbsp. Paprika
2 Large Onions	1/2 Cup Hot Chili Powder
1 Tbsp. Cumin	1 Cup Olive Oil
1/4 Cup Corn Flour	Salt to Taste
5 Long Dried Chilies	2 Tbsp. Oregano

Clean dried chilies by removing seeds and stems, then chop.

Heat beer and add spices.

In large pot, saute pork and beef in olive oil until all sides are brown.

Add onions and saute until transparent.

Add beer, spices and chilies to meat.

In separate small bowl, mix corn flour with small amount of water. Add to chili.

Bring to boil and simmer for about 2 hours or until meat is tender and chili is thick.

Add more corn flour if too thin.

Serves 8.

BEER QUIZ QUESTION 4

What quality does yeast impart to beer?

A) Sweetness
B) Freshness
C) Dryness
D) Fruitiness

ED'S BEER BATTER CHICKEN

3/4 CUP BEER	3/4 Cup Flour
2 1/2 Lb. Frying Chicken	3/4 Tsp. Salt
2 Eggs, Separated	1 1/2 Tsp. Vegetable Oil
3 Tbsp. Frying Oil	1/4 Tsp. Garlic Powder

Let beer stand at room temperature until flat (about 45 minutes).

Cut chicken into pieces, cutting each breast in half. Place chicken in Dutch oven and pour enough water over chicken just to cover.

Heat to boiling, reduce temperature, cover and simmer for 25 minutes.

Remove chicken pieces from pan, drain and pat dry.

Heat frying oil in kettle or deep fryer to 375 degrees.

Beat egg whites until stiff.

In separate bowl, beat beer, flour, salt, 1 1/2 tsp. oil, garlic and egg yolks until smooth. Fold egg whites into mixture.

Dip chicken pieces, one at a time, into batter. Drop 3 or 4 pieces in hot oil for 5 to 7 minutes or until golden brown.

Serves 2 to 4.

BUBBA'S FRIED CHICKEN

2/3 CUP BEER	2 Tbsp. Oil
2 Eggs, well beaten	1 Broiler-Fryer Chicken, quartered
1 Cup Flour	1 Qt. Oil for frying
	1/2 Tsp. Salt

Combine eggs and beer. Slowly beat in flour, salt and oil until batter is smooth. Dip chicken into batter; drain. Drop Into heated oil at 275 degrees and fry for 15 to 20 minutes.. Serves 2.

This basic beer batter serves equally well for Shrimp Tempura. Don't forget to add 1/2 teaspoon of ginger. Coats 2 pounds of unshelled shrimp.

BEER BATTERED FRIED SHRIMP

1 CAN BEER
2 Lbs. Medium Shrimp
1 Cup Flour

1 1/2 Tsp. Salt
1/8 Tsp. Crushed Red Pepper
1 Quart Frying Oil

Clean shrimp.

Combine in large bowl: beer, flour, salt and pepper until smooth.

Dip shrimp into batter and drop in hot oil (use either large skillet or deep-fryer) until golden brown.

Drain on paper towel.

Serves 6.

SHRIMP DUNK

16 OZ. BEER
2 Small Sliced Onions
1 Clove Garlic
1 Bay Leaf

2 Whole Stalks Celery
1 1/2 Tsp. Salt
2 Lbs. Raw, Unshelled Shrimp
1/2 Lemon

Put all ingredients except shrimp into large pot. Bring to boil.

Add shrimp and simmer for 10 minutes.

Allow shrimp to cool in beer.

Peel off shells.

Chill well.

Serve with one deep dunking bowl of ice cold beer.

BEER BOILED SHRIMP

Shell and devein shrimp before cooking.

Drop shrimp into boiling beer and wafer, using 2 parts stale beer to 1 part water.

Use 1 tablespoon salt for each quart liquid, a few peppercorns, 1 or 2 bay leaves, and a sprinkling of celery seed.

Simmer, covered, for 2 to 5 minutes, or until shrimp are pink.

Drain, cool, and serve.

No sauce is needed when shrimp are cooked this way.

COME AND GET IT CATFISH

1 CUP LIGHT BEER
2 Lbs. Farm Grown Catfish
  Fillets
4 Cups Flour
1 Tbsp. Baking Powder

1 Tsp. Paprika
1/4 Cup Milk
1/2 Cup Water (Very cold)
3 Egg Whites, Beaten until Stiff
2 Tsp. Salt

Coat fillets lightly with half the flour.

Mix the remaining flour (2 cups) with the baking powder, paprika and salt.

In a separate bowl, mix beer, milk, and cold water.

Fold in egg whites.

Add beer mixture to dry ingredients and stir slightly.

Meat oil in large skillet. Dip fillets in beer batter and place in skillet.

Fry until golden brown.

Serves 4.

BEER QUIZ QUESTION 5

What do beer vendors shout in Russia?

A) Itti Bikka!

B) Kvass!

C) Yokschka!

D) lach Pivo!

MARINATED SWORDFISH

Combine 4 CUPS BEER, 1/2 cup salt, 1/2 cup brown sugar, 1 teaspoon pepper, 1 teaspoon coriander seed, 2 teaspoons allspice, 1 bay leaf and 1 whole clove.

Place mixture in saucepan and bring to boil.

Lower heat and simmer for 20 minutes.

Cool.

Marinate 2 pounds sword fish steaks in mixture for 3 hours in refrigerator.

Cook steak on aluminum foil on barbecue or grill in broiler until fish just gently flakes.

ANYTHING GOES JAMBALAYA

1/2 CUP LIGHT BEER	2 Cups White Rice, uncooked
4 Cups Beef Broth	1/2 Cup Oil
2 Large Tomatoes, Chopped	2 Large Onion Chopped
1 Lb. Large Shrimp, Cleaned	2 Celery Stalks, Chopped
2 Lbs. Smoked Sausage	12 Scallions, Chopped
2 Medium Bell Peppers, Chopped	7 Cloves Garlic, Thinly Sliced
1 Lb. Ham, Diced in Chunks	1 Tsp. Crushed Red Pepper

In large fry pan, heat oil. Add onion, bell pepper, garlic and hot pepper. Saute, stirring, about 5 minutes. Add sausage and ham and cook for 5 minutes.

In a large Dutch oven, brown rice in oil.

Add remaining ingredients except shrimp. Cover and simmer for 45 minutes.

Add shrimp and cook for 5 minutes. Remove from heat and let stand for 10 minutes.

Add dried parsley for garnish.

Serves 8 to 10.

SAN ANTONIO TACOS

1/2 CUP BEER	2 Tbsp. Wine Vinegar
1 (1 3/8 oz.) Envelope	3 Drops Tabasco (or to taste)
Dehydrated Onion Soup Mix	4 Pkgs. Frozen Cocktail Tacos
1/2 Cup Chili Sauce	(about 48)

Combine onion soup mix with sour cream.

Stir in beer, chili sauce, vinegar and Tabasco. Chill until ready to serve. Heat tacos according to package directions.

Serve hot with the dip.

HEADY HONEYDEW DESSERT

Peel 2 large oranges and separate wedges.

In medium sauce pan pour the juice of 1 large jar maraschino cherries.

Add 1/2 cup orange juice, 1/2 cup sugar and 3 tablespoons of BEER.

Cover over medium heat, stirring constantly, until mixture thickens slightly.

Add the oranges and unstemmed cherries. Cook for 2 minutes.

Cool.

Cut one very ripe honeydew melon into 4 slices. Place each slice on a dessert plate.

Just before serving, add 1/4 cup blueberries to fruit mixture.

Place fruit over melon slice.

Serves 4.

BEER QUIZ QUESTION 6

Which country consumes the most beer?

A) U.S.A.
B) Germany
C) Australia
D) Japan

SWEET STOUT CHEESECAKE

CRUST

1 1/2 Cups All Purpose Flour	2 Medium Eggs
1/2 Cup Sugar	1 Tsp. Vanilla Extract
1/2 Tsp. Salt	5 Tbsps. Cold Butter, cut in pieces

In food processor, mix dry ingredients. Drop in butter pieces until soft dough consistency.

Roll into ball.

Lightly press dough into greased 10 inch spring form pan, forming a thin crust on bottom of pan and sides of pan.

Flute edges.

FILLING

1/2 CUP SWEET BEER	1 1/2 Cups Heavy Cream
2 (1 1/4 oz.) Pkgs. Cream Cheese	1 Cup Unsweetened Cocoa
2 Cups Sugar	1/2 Cup Melted Butter
1 Tsp. Vanilla Extract	1 Tsp. Almond Extract
6 Large Eggs	

Preheat oven to 225 degrees.

Beat cream cheese, sugar, vanilla and almond extract in mixer until sugar is dissolved.

Add eggs and beat on low until just mixed. Stir remaining ingredients into mixture with spoon.

Pour into crust and bake for 1 hour or until center is set. Test with thin knife.

Turn off oven and let cheesecake stay inside until cool.

For added touch, sprinkle top with chopped almonds and serve with whipped cream.

BAKLAVA BALLYHOO

FILLING

4 Cups Chopped Mixed Nuts, Toasted	3/4 Cup Brown Sugar
	2 Tbsps. Cinnamon
1/4 Cup Toasted Sesame Seeds	1/4 Cup Sugar

For dough use 2 pounds of phyllo sheets and 2 pounds of unsalted, clarified butter.

Combine all ingredients in bowl and set aside.

Place a sheet of phyllo on a lightly greased cookie sheet. Brush the top with melted butter.

Place a small amount of filling on the phyllo sheet and roll carefully, Form a tube and wrap into a coil.

Continue making small coils.

Cover cookie sheet with a damp towel as you work so that the Baklava does not dry out.

Preheat oven to 350 degrees. Bake for 35 to 45 minutes or until golden brown.

SYRUP FOR BAKLAVA

1 CUP ALE	2 Tsp. Cinnamon
1 1/2 Cups Water	1 Tbsp. Grated Lemon Zest
1 1/2 Cups Sugar	1/4 Cup Lemon Juice
3/4 Cup Brown Sugar	1 Cup Corn Syrup

Place all ingredients in sauce pan and bring to boil.

Quickly reduce heat and simmer uncovered for 35 minutes.

Cool before pouring over Baklava.

Do not serve before pastry stands for at least 4 hours.

BEER QUIZ QUESTION 7

What kind of taste does malt give to beer?

A) Sweet
B) Sour
C) Bitter
D) Salty

ANSWERS TO BEER QUIZ

1) D - Bavaria

2) A - Hops

3) C - Ten Ounces

4) D - Fruitiness

5) B - Kvass!

6) B - Germany

7) A - Sweet

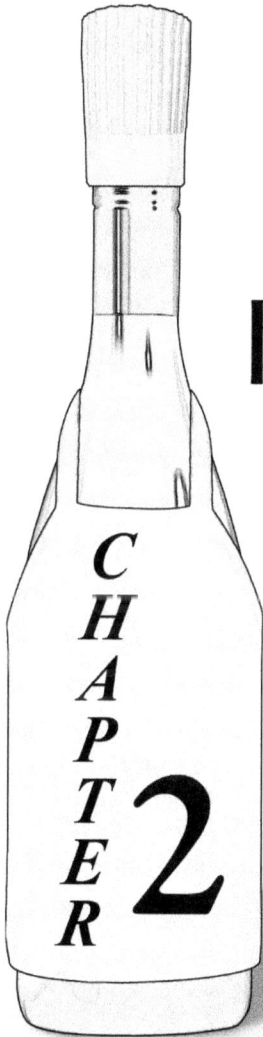

Fine Dining with WINE

C H A P T E R 2

Cooking with WINE is a science, an art, and a tradition.

WINE used in cooking is much more than just a flavoring. It is a blender and enhancer of flavors. WINE accents the savoriness of food and lends both aroma and smoothness.

There is a use in cookery for almost every WINE - appetizer, red table, white table, dessert and even sparkling wines.

CHEESE FONDUE A LA ALLY

1 CUP WHITE WINE
1 Clove Garlic, halved
1 1/2 Cups Grated Gruyere
1 ½ Cups Grated Emmental
Pinch Nutmeg

2 Tsp. Cornstarch
1 Tsp. Fresh Lemon Juice
Splash of Cherry Brandy
Freshly Ground Pepper to taste

Rub inside of fondue pot with garlic halves.

Mix together Gruyere, Emmental and cornstarch.

Add wine, lemon juice, cherry brandy, pepper and nutmeg.

Heat mixture. When hot, not boiling, add cheese, a handful at a time. Stir with a wooden spoon.

Wait for each portion of cheese to melt before adding more.

Serve with plenty of crusty bread.

Enjoy!

CREAM CHEESE BONAPARTE

1/2 CUP WHITE WINE
1 Lb. Cream Cheese

2 Tsp. Lime Juice
1/4 Cup Sugar

In blender, slowly mix cheese and sugar until smooth.

Pour in wine and juice and blend until mixed.

Place in fancy serving bowl and surround with crackers of your choice.

DEVILED BEEF STEW

1/2 CUP DRY WHITE WINE   4 Carrots

1 Lb. Beef Bottom Round Steak   2 Potatoes

2 Tbsp. Mustard   1 Cup Fat Skimmed Beef Broth

2 Tsp. Worcestershire Sauce   2 Stalks Celery

2 Tbsp. Flour   1/4 Cup Cold Water

8 Small Onions

Cut meat into 1 inch cubes, trim and discard fat.

Stir cubes with mustard and Worcestershire until well coated.

Arrange cubes in single layer in non-stick skillet, well sprayed with cooking spray.

Brown meat slowly with no fat added, turning to brown evenly.

Drain and discard any fat.

Add broth and wine. Cover tightly and simmer until meat is nearly tender, 1 hour or more.

Meanwhile, peel small onions. Pare carrots and potatoes and slice carrots, celery into 3 inch lengths.

Cut potatoes into thick 3/4 inch slices.

Skim any fat from liquid in pan.

Add vegetables.

Cover and simmer until vegetables are tender, about 20 to 25 minutes.

Combine flour with 1/4 cup of water and stir into simmering liquid until thickened.

Serves 4.

EGGS IN LUSH MUSHROOM SAUCE

1 CUP DRY WHITE WINE
1/2 Cup Margarine
1/2 Lb. Small Mushrooms, sliced
1 1/4 Cup Chicken Broth
Salt & Pepper to Taste

2 Scallions, chopped
6 Eggs
4 Tbsp. Sour Cream
1/2 Cup Mild Cheddar Cheese,
  grated

Place margarine in hot skillet. When melted, add sliced mushroom and saute until slightly brown.

Mix in flour and gradually add wine and broth. On low heat add sour cream slowly, stirring constantly until smooth. Mix in scallions, salt and pepper to taste.

Pour mushroom mixture into six 3 inch round baking dishes and break one egg into center of each dish. Cover top with a little melted butter or margarine and sprinkle with cheese.

Bake in preheated 400 degree oven for about 8 minutes or until eggs are set. Garnish with chopped parsley.

Serves 6.

WINE QUIZ QUESTION 1

According to the Bible, who invented wine?

A) Adam
B) Moses
C) Noah
D) Satan

VEAL MILANESE

1 1/2 CUPS DRY WHITE WINE
7 Slices Veal Shanks, 5 to 6 lbs.,
  cut 2 inches thick
Salt and Pepper
2 Tbsp. Olive Oil
Flour for Dredging
9 Tbsp. Finely minced Garlic

1 1/2 Cups Finely Chopped Onion
1/2 Cup Chopped Celery
1 Cup Chopped Carrots
2 Cups Peeled, Crushed Tomatoes
1/4 Cup Chopped Parsley
1 Tsp. Crushed Marjoram

Sprinkle veal with pepper and salt and dredge in flour, removing excess. In a heavy skillet sufficiently large to hold veal with bone upright, in single layer, heat oil. Brown for 30 minutes on all sides.

Add the carrots, celery, and onion. Cook about 15 minutes, stirring. Add marjoram and garlic. Stir, then add wine. Cook another minute, then add tomatoes. Pepper and salt to taste. Cover and cook 1 hour and 15 minutes. Sprinkle with chopped parsley and serve with rice.

Serves 6.

TENDERLOIN TIPS IN WINE

1 CUP BURGUNDY WINE
1 Lb. Beef Tenderloin,
  cut in 1/4 strips
2 Medium Onions, Chopped
2 Med. Green Peppers, Chopped

6 Tbsp. Butter or Margarine
1/2 Tsp. Black Pepper
1 Can Brown Gravy
2 Tbsp. Com Starch
Hot Cooked Rice

Melt 2 Tbsp. butter or margarine in large skillet. Add tenderloins and saute until brown. Remove meat and set aside.

Melt 4 Tbsp.butter or margarine in skillet, add onion, green pepper, salt and pepper to taste. Saute 3 minutes, stir in gravy. Combine wine and cornstarch, mix well. Pour into pan. Cook on medium heat until bubbling, stirring constantly. Cook on low heat for 2 minutes, stirring occasionally. Add meat, stirring well. Serve over rice.

Serves 4.

LANCER MEAT LOAF

1/4 CUP DRY RED WINE
2 Lbs. Ground Chuck
1 Tbsp. Worcestershire Sauce
1 Small Onion
1 Large egg, beaten
3/4 Cup Beef Stock or Broth

3 Tbsp. Tomato Sauce
1 Cup Italian Seasoned Bread
    Crumbs
1 Tbsp. Steak Sauce
Salt and Pepper to taste

Combine all ingredients.

Pack in meat loaf pan and bake in 350 degree oven for 1 hour.

Remove from oven, baste off juices.

Serves 7 to 8.

WINE QUIZ QUESTION 2

The consistency of wine is referred to as its....

A) Body
B) Heart
C) Soul
D) Character

TUSCANY BRAISED POT ROAST

2 CUPS RED WINE	2 Cloves Garlic
2 Lbs. Top Round, Boned	1 Cup Italian Parsley, Chopped
1 Medium Onion, Chopped	3 Cups Beef Stock or Broth
1 Carrot, Chopped	4 Tbsp. Olive Oil
1 Stalk Celery, Chopped	3 Oz. Golden Raisins
2 Oz. Toasted Pine Nuts	2 Oz. Dried Figs
2 Oz. Toasted Sliced Almonds	1/2 Tsp. Red Pepper Flakes

Heat 2 Tbsp. olive oil in heavy Dutch oven. Saute finely chopped onion, carrot and celery until soft. Sprinkle red pepper flakes on top and stir well.

With a slotted spoon remove solids from pan and reserve. Leave any remaining oil in pan for later.

Prepare stuffing mixture by chopping together in the food processor the garlic, nuts, raisins, figs and parsley, until all ingredients hold together. Do not over process.

With a sharp knife, make slits here and there all over the roast. Insert a tsp. of stuffing mixture in each slit. Reserve the remaining mixture. Tie the roast securely with kitchen string into a nice oblong shape.

Return pan to moderate heat and add remaining 2 Tbsp. olive oil. Heat well. Add roast and brown on all sides. Add the wine and 2 cups of the beef stock or broth. Move roast about while scraping bottom of Dutch oven to deglaze any brown bits. Add remaining nut mixture to sauce.

The liquids should barely cover the meat. Simmer on low, covered for about 2 hours. Add more stock if necessary.

Remove meat from pan, and let cool for 15 minutes.

While meat is cooling, return pan to heat to reduce the sauce.

Slice meat thinly and drizzle sauce on top.

Serve with buttered flat noodles or polenta.

Serves 5.

CROCK POT BEEF STEW

3/4 CUP DRY RED WINE
1 1/2 Lbs. Beef Stew Meat
1 8 oz. Can Tomato Sauce
3/4 Cup Water
2 Cups Sliced Potato Wedges
with Peel

1 Tsp. Bottled Chopped Garlic
1 16 oz. Pkg. Loose Packed Frozen
Mixed Broccoli, Cauliflower, and
Carrots (4 Cups)

In 3 quart electric crock pot, combine all ingredients except vegetables. Cook on low setting for 8 to 10 hours or on high setting for 4 to 5 hours. At serving time, cook vegetables and potatoes in boiling water for about 15 minutes or until potatoes are just tender.

Skim off fat from stew and serve over vegetables.

Serves 6.

BEEF AND BACON BURGUNDY

1/4 CUP BURGUNDY
4 Slices Bacon
1 Can Golden Mushroom Soup
1 1/2 Lbs. Top Round, Cubed

2 Tbsp. Dried Parsley
1/8 Tsp. Black Pepper
12 Small Whole Onions
2 Cups Sliced Mushrooms

Cook bacon until crisp in large pan. Remove and crumble.

Brown beef in drippings and pour off fat.

Add soup, wine, parsley and pepper. Cover and cook over low heat for 1 1/2 hours.

Add onions and mushrooms, cover and cook 1 hour more.

Garnish with bacon and serve over noodles.

Serves 4.

NO-PEEK BEEF CASSEROLE

1/2 CUP RED WINE
2 Lbs. Beef, cut in 1" Cubes
1 Envelope Onion Soup Mix
1 Cup Sour Cream

1 10 1/2 oz. Can Cream of
  Mushroom Soup
1 4 oz. Can Sliced Mushrooms
1/3 Cup Flour

Combine all ingredients in crock pot.

Stir together well.

Cover and cook on low for 8 to 12 hours or on high for 5 to 6 hours.

Serve over noodles or rice.

Serves 4 to 6.

BEEF PATTIES DIJON

1/4 CUP WHITE WINE
1 Lb. Ground Chuck or Round
3 Tbsp. Butter or Margarine
1/2 Lb. Sliced Mushrooms

2 Green onions, Sliced
2 Tbsp. Water
2 Tbsp. Dijon Mustard
Salt and Pepper to Taste

Salt and pepper beef and shape into four patties.

Cook patties in large fry pan until brown and remove to platter.

In drippings melt butter or margarine, mushrooms and green onion and cook until tender.

Stir in wine, water, mustard and 1/4 tsp. salt.

Return patties to pan and heat thoroughly, stirring frequently.

Serves 4.

BEEF BURGERS
WITH BLUE CHEESE SAUCE

1/2 Cup RED or WHITE WINE	2 Tbsp. Virgin Olive Oil
8 to 12 Oz. Ground Beef	1/2 Cup Heavy Cream
Salt & Pepper to Taste	4 Tbsp. Butter or Margarine
1/8 Tsp. Thyme	4 Tbsp. Crumbled Blue Cheese
1/8 Tsp. Rosemary	

Lightly mix beef, salt, pepper, thyme and rosemary in bowl. Form two 1 inch patties.

In medium medium fry pan, heat oil until hot. Place patties in pan and brown both sides. Lower heat and cook until meat is cooked through.

Remove patties from pan and keep warm.

Pour off fat from pan and add wine. Bring wine to a rolling boil until only 1 tablespoon remains. It will be just a glaze on the bottom.

Add cream and stir rapidly until mixture begins to boil. Continue stirring for 1 and 1/2 minutes. Sauce should be thick and syrupy.

Remove from heat and whisk in butter or margarine about 1 tablespoon at a time, letting each piece melt.

Stir in the cheese, letting It warm through. Do not completely melt cheese.

Pour sauce over patties and serve immediately.

Serves 2.

Variation:

Omit cheese and add 8 to 12 mushrooms, sliced and browned in butter.

LAZY BEEF CASSEROLE

1/2 CUP RED WINE	1/8 Tsp. Pepper
1 Lb. Cubed Stew Meat	1 Med. Onion, Chopped
1 Can Consomme, undiluted	1/4 Cup Bread Crumbs
3/4 Tsp. Salt	1/4 Cup Flour

Preheat oven to 300 degrees. Place meat into casserole dish with the wine, consomme, seasonings and onion. Mix flour and bread crumbs and stir into liquid. Cover and bake for 3 hours. Can be served with rice or noodles.

Serves 4.

HUNGRY HUNGARIAN'S GOULASH

1/4 CUP DRY WHITE WINE	1/2 Tsp. Caraway Seeds
1 Lb. Beef Bottom Round	1 Bay Leaf
1 Cup Sliced Onions	2 Potatoes, Peeled and Sliced
2 Tbsp. Water	4 Tsp. Minced Fresh Parsley
8 Oz. Can Stewed Tomatoes	1 Tsp. Paprika
1 Cup Beef Broth	Salt and Pepper to Taste

Spray non-stick Dutch oven with cooking spray. Trim off any fat on beef and cut into 1 and 1/2 inch cubes. Add to pot. Brown slowly over moderate heat with no fat added; turn to brown evenly. Discard any melted fat from pot. Stir in onions and water. Cook and stir until onions are transparent. Add tomatoes and stir until broken up well. Add broth, wine, caraway, bay leaf, salt and pepper. Cover tightly and simmer over very low heat until meat is nearly tender, 1 and 1/2 hours or more. (Add a little water, if needed.) Skim any fat from surface of liquid. Add potatoes; cover and simmer about 20 minutes until potatoes are just tender. Uncover and simmer until sauce is thick. Discard bay leaf. Spoon goulash onto serving plates and top each portion with a dollop of sour cream or yogurt, if desired. Sprinkle with parsley and paprika.

Serves 4.

TEN MINUTE CHICKEN PAPRIKASH WITH NOODLES

1/2 CUP DRY SHERRY	2 Tbsp. Minced Fresh Parsley
8 Oz. Wide Noodles	1/2 Cup Part-Skim Ricotta Cheese
4 Boneless Chicken Breasts	Salt and Pepper to Taste
or 2 Whole Chicken Breasts	Pinch of Red Cayenne Pepper
1 Sweet Onion	1 Tbsp. Sweet Paprika
1/2 Lb. Small Fresh Mushrooms	

Cook noodles in boiling salted water according to package directions.

Meanwhile, cut chicken cutlets into bite-size cubes.

Cut peeled onion in half, then thinly slice.

Leave mushrooms whole (large mushrooms may be sliced).

Combine ricotta and parsley in food processor or blender and puree completely smooth.

Spray a large non stick skillet with cooking spray. Arrange the chicken cubes in a single layer.

Cook uncovered, over moderate heat until underside is lightly browned; turn to brown evenly.

Stir in onion and wine. Simmer over moderate heat until onions are tender-crunchy, about three minutes.

Stir in mushrooms until heated through and most of the wine has evaporated, 1 or 2 minutes. Remove from heat.

Season to taste with salt, pepper and cayenne.

Stir in ricotta mixture, until chicken and mushrooms are coated with a thick sauce.

Spoon over hot drained noodles and sprinkle liberally with paprika before serving.

Serves 6.

BREASTS AND WINE
AND HAVE A GOOD TIME

1 lb. Spaghettini No. 9 or any Thin Spaghetti

2 Lg. Boneless, Skinless Chicken Breasts

1 Pkg. Frozen Broccoli Rosettes (fresh broccoli can be used but must be flash boiled *)

1 Cup Sliced Sun Dried Tomatoes (do not use tomatoes in oil)

1 Tbs. Chopped, Fresh Garlic

1 Cup Dry White Wine

Olive Oil

Salt to taste

*To flash boil broccoli, place in boiling water for one minute. Quickly remove and place in bowl of ice water. The broccoli with be very green and will keep in refrigerator for a week.

MARINADE

½ Cup Balsamic Vinegar	1 Tsp. Oregano
¼ Cup Olive Oil	½ Tsp. Salt
2 Tsp. Garlic Powder	

It is best to marinade chicken breasts overnight. Mix all ingredients together and pour over chicken breasts. Place in refrigerator covered, turning chicken over once.

Cook chicken either on the barbecue or in a grilling pan until firm when pressed with a fork and dark brown in color. Do not overcook. If chicken is slightly pink, it will finish cooking in skillet.

When cold, slice chicken breasts on the diagonal into approximately ½ inch slices.

Bring large pot of water to a rolling boil. Add 1 tsp. of salt and pasta. Gently push pasta down into the pot and stir to avoid sticking together. Cook for 11 minutes.

(Continued on next page)

Put 2 tbs. of olive oil in large skillet. Oil must be hot but not smoking.

Add cold, sliced chicken breasts, sun dried tomatoes and broccoli to pan. Saute ingredients until hot and slightly browned, about 4 minutes or until chicken is completely done.

Add garlic and salt to taste.

Lower heat and cook until garlic is brown.

Keep stirring with thongs while cooking.

Add wine and raise heat to medium/high. Reduce wine and scrape the bottom of the skillet until wine is thicker and dark in color.

Place pasta in serving dish and pour about 1 tbs. of olive oil over it. Mix. Then place chicken mixture over pasta.

Sprinkle top with parmesan/Romano cheese and parsley.

Italian red pepper flakes can also be added for a bit of heat.

Extra olive oil can also be added for heartier flavor.

This dish will serve 4 people.

WINE QUIZ QUESTION 3

You should not drink wine while eating...

A) Spicy Food
B) Chinese Food
C) Chocolate
D) Any of the above

CHICKEN HULA

1 TBSP. SWEET SHERRY
1 JIGGER ORANGE LIQUEUR
1 Cup Duck Sauce
1/4 Tsp. Ginger
1/2 Cup Barbecue Sauce

1 Can Mandarin Oranges
1 Can Pineapple Chunks
2 Small Chickens, Cut in Pieces
1 Small Can Frozen Pineapple
  Juice

Mix all ingredients except oranges and pineapple chunks.

Marinate chicken pieces in mixture overnight.

Preheat oven to 275 degrees and bake chicken for one hour.

Drain pineapple and oranges and place over chicken and bake another half hour.

Serves 6.

CHEF CONRAD'S CHICKEN SAVOY

1 CUP RED WINE
3 Cups Wine Vinegar
16 to 20 Pieces Chicken
2 Cups Chicken Broth

1 Entire Bulb of Garlic, Minced
1 Tbsp. Fresh Basil
1 1/2 Cups Parmesan Cheese

Mix wine and vinegar together, set aside.

Place chicken, skin up in a large baking pan. Pour 1/2 of vinegar mixture and 1/2 chicken broth over the chicken pieces. Generously sprinkle the garlic, basil and grated cheese over the chicken.

Place In preheated 350 degree oven. After 30 minutes, pour off vinegar mixture into a saucepan and replace with a new mixture and proceed as before. Do this again after another 30 minutes.

Skim off the chicken fat and thicken sauce. Lightly sprinkle vinegar on chicken and place under broiler for a few minutes.

Serve with sauce on the side. Serves 6.

CHICKEN EN CIVET

1/2 CUP WHITE WINE	Pinch of Ground Cloves
2 Lbs. Cut-up Frying Chicken	1 or 2 Small Bay Leaves
3 Tbsp. Flour	1/4 Tsp. Thyme
6 Oz. Canadian Bacon, Diced	Salt and Pepper to Taste
10 Oz. Can Undiluted Chicken Broth	1 Medium Onion, Chopped

Preheat oven to 475 degrees.

Meanwhile, spray a non-stick roasting pan liberally with cooking spray.

Arrange the chopped onion and diced bacon on the bottom of the pan.

Season the flour with salt and pepper in a large grocery bag. Add the chicken pieces a few at a time and shake up until lightly coated.

Arrange the chicken pieces skin side up in the roasting pan, covering the onion and diced bacon.

Put the pan in the hot oven, uncovered, and let the chicken brown 15 to 20 minutes.

Remove the pan from the oven. Pour the wine and chicken broth around, not over, the chicken.

Cover and return the pan to the oven.

Lower the heat to 350 degrees. Bake covered 40 to 45 minutes, until chicken is tender.

Serve with the pan juices spooned over.

Remove bay leaves before serving.

Serves 6.

CHICKEN ROLLETTES FLORENTINE

1/2 CUP CHABLIS
2 Lbs. Chicken Cutlets
3/4 Cup Italian Seasoned
   Bread Crumbs
1/2 Cup Mozzarella Cheese,
   Shredded

8 Oz. Can Plain Tomato Sauce
10 Oz. Pkg. Frozen Chopped
   Spinach, Defrosted
1 Egg, Lightly Beaten
1/2 Cup Chopped Onion
1 or 2 Cloves of Garlic, Minced

Flatten chicken. Combine spinach, bread crumbs, cheese and egg. Spread mixture over cutlets. Roll with filling inside and place with seam-side down in non-stick baking dish. Combine tomato sauce, wine, onion and garlic, pour over chicken. Cover with foil; bake in 350 degree oven for 1 and 1/2 hours or until chicken is tender. Uncover during last 20 minutes to let sauce reduce. To serve, spoon on sauce.

Serves 8.

CHICKEN IN WINE & ROSEMARY

2/3 CUP DRY WHITE WINE
1 Tbsp. Olive Oil
1 Glove Garlic, Crushed
3 1/2 Lb. Chicken, cut up

1 Tbsp. Rosemary
1/2 Tsp. Salt
1/2 Cup Wine Vinegar
2 Tbsp. Butter or Margarine

25 minutes before serving, heat oil in large frying pan. Saute garlic until golden brown. Do not overcook. Discard garlic. In same pan cook chicken until well browned on all sides. Add rosemary, salt and wine vinegar. Cover immediately. When vinegar stops sizzling (2 to 3 minutes) add wine. Reduce heat, cover and simmer 20 minutes or until chicken is fork tender.

To serve, remove chicken to serving dish. Keep warm over high heat. Heat sauce to boiling. With spoon loosen brown bits in pan. Stir in butter until melted. Spoon over chicken.

Serves 4.

CHICKEN A LA SUSIE

1/2 CUP WHITE WINE	1 Tsp. Paprika
6 Chicken Breasts, Boned & Skinned	6 Tbsp. Butter or Margarine
	1 Chicken Bullion Cube
8 Oz. Swiss Cheese	1 Tbsp. Cornstarch
3 Tbsp. Flour	1 Cup Heavy Cream
8 Oz. Sliced Ham	

Spread chicken breasts flat. Cut cheese and ham to fit on top of chicken. Fold breasts over filling and fasten sides with toothpicks.

Mix Paprika and flour. Coat breasts lightly with flour mixture.

In 12" skillet, heat butter and add breasts. Cook chicken until golden brown on all sides.

Add wine and bullion. Reduce heat to low, cover and simmer for 30 minutes.

Remove chicken from skillet and keep warm.

Blend cornstarch and cream until smooth. Gradually stir into liquid in skillet. Cook mixture, stirring constantly until thick.

Spoon over chicken and serve. Serves 6.

WINE QUIZ QUESTION 4

A novice wine taster is encouraged to...

A) Study Labels
B) Travel to France
C) Use a Flute Glass
D) Drink a Lot

SHARON'S CHICKEN PARISIENNE

1/2 CUP VERMOUTH

Salt and Pepper

Paprika

1 Cup Sour Cream

1 Chicken, Cut in Pieces

1 Can Cream of Mushroom Soup

14 Oz. Can Sliced Mushrooms, Drained (1/2 Cup)

1/4 Cup Flour

Sprinkle chicken lightly with salt, pepper and paprika. Place in crock pot. Mix vermouth, soup and mushrooms until well combined. Pour over chicken.

Combine flour and sour cream. Add to chicken.

Cook on high for 2 1/2 to 3 hours. If cooking on low, do not add sour cream mixture until last 30 minutes. Cook chicken on low for 6 to 8 hours.

Serves 3 to 4.

DEVILISH CHICKEN CHESTS

1 CUP DRY WHITE WINE

2 Split Frying Chicken Breasts

Several Bay Leaves

2 Tbsp. Spicy Brown Mustard

Pinch of Dried Thyme

Dash of Ground Nutmeg

Brown chicken pieces skin-side up under broiler until skin is crisp and well rendered of fat, about 10 minutes. Discard melted fat.

Arrange bay leaves in bottom of non-stick baking dish and place browned chicken pieces on top. Combine remaining ingredients in covered far and shake well. Pour over chicken. Bake at 350 degrees for 20 to 25 minutes, or until chicken is cooked through, basting occasionally with mustard sauce that forms in pan.

Discard bay leaves before serving.

Serves 4.

CHICKEN A LA LONNY

1/2 CUP DRY WHITE WINE   Generous Pinch of Thyme
8 Chicken Thighs   Salt and Pepper to Taste
1 Tbsp. Spicy Brown Mustard   1 Small Bay Leaf
4 Medium Onions

Place the chicken skin-side up in a single layer in a shallow non-stick pan. Place under broiler until skin is crisp and rendered of fat. Turn to brown evenly.
Drain and discard fat.

While chicken is browning, combine remaining ingredients, except onions, in a covered jar and shake up well to blend. Pour over chicken.

Cut onions in half and add.

Cover the pan loosely with foil and bake at 250 degrees for 20 to 25 minutes. Uncover pan and continue to bake uncovered, basting and turning chicken often, until chicken is tender and most of the liquid has evaporated into a thick, flavorful glaze.

Serves 4.

WINE QUIZ QUESTION 5

What does a dry wine lack?

A) Sugar
B) Tartness
C) Alcohol
D) Body

DUCK BREASTS IN LINGONBERRIES AND RED WINE

2 TBSP. RED WINE	**1/2 Tsp. Olive Oil**
2 Whole Duck Breasts, Boned	**1 Cup Chicken Broth**
(About 3/4 to 1 Lb. Each)	**1/2 Cup Lingonberries**
Course Salt & Pepper to Taste	

On a work surface, cut duck breasts in half lengthwise.

Trim any extra fat and skin from around the meat on each breast. With a sharp knife, score the skin 2 times diagonally without piercing the meat.

Sprinkle all over with salt and pepper.

Brush 1 large or 2 medium size non-stick skillets with olive oil. Place the breasts, skin-side down, in the skillet over high heat.

Saute, pressing down on the breasts, with the back of a spatula until they are well browned, about 5 to 6 minutes, for rare meat.

If the pan gets too hot, reduce the heat to medium.

Remove the breasts to a plate and cover to keep warm until serving. Pour off fat and repeat with the remaining breasts.

Discard all the fat in the pan and wipe it out with a paper towel.

Place the skillet over medium heat. Add broth along with any duck juices that accumulated in the plate.

Boil 1 minute, reduce heat to medium and stir in the Lingonberries and wine.

Cook for about 7 minutes or until slightly thickened, stirring occasionally.

To serve, slice the warm duck breasts thinly on the diagonal. Pan the slices out on a serving platter and spoon the warm sauce over the top.

Serve immediately.

Serves 6 to 8.

CECILIA'S CODFISH WITH PORT

¾ CUP PORT
2 Lb. Codfish
Olive Oil
1 Lg. Red Onion, Sliced
3 Garlic Cloves

4 Tomatoes, Sliced in small pieces
Green & Red Peppers, 1 each,
 Sliced
1 Can Kalamatas (black olives)
Parsley, Basil and Salt & Pepper

Salsa: In a quarter inch of olive oil in a sauce pan fry the onions and garlic, then stir in the tomatoes, green & red peppers slices & the kalamatas. Season with parsley, basil, salt and black pepper.

Fry the codfish in a separate buttered pan for about 5 minutes or until fish is white and flakes when parted with a fork. Do not overcook.

Add port and serve with a generous helping of the salsa.

Serves 4 to 6.

FANCY-FREE FILLET OF SOLE WITH MUSHROOMS

1/4 CUP DRY WHITE WINE
1 Onion, Diced
2 Cups Sliced Mushrooms
1 Tsp. Vegetable Oil
1 1/4 Lbs. Fillet of Sole

2 Tbsp. Lemon Juice
2 Tbsb. Fresh Chopped Parsley
1/2 Tsp. Oregano
1/8 Tsp. Black Pepper

Saute onion and sliced mushrooms in oil, using a non-stick skillet. Stir until tender. Lay fillets in skillet. Add wine, lemon juice and parsley. Sprinkle fillets with oregano and pepper. Cover and simmer over low heat for 10 minutes, or until fish flakes easily.

Serves 4.

LOLA'S POACHED SALMON IN WINE

1 CUP DRY WHITE WINE	2 Tbls. Butter
1/4 Cup Water	1 Tsp. Salt
1 Lb. Salmon Fillet	1/8 Tsp. Black Pepper
(Cut in Half)	1 Tsp. Dried Dill Powder
1 Tomato, sliced thick	1 Small Onion, Sliced in Rounds

Place salmon fillet in large skillet, skin side down. Add wine, water, butter, salt, pepper and dried dill powder. Place slices of tomato and onion on top of fish. Bring to a boil. Reduce heat, cover and simmer for about 7 minutes or until salmon loses its pink color and gently flakes. Remove fish from pan and place on serving dish. Sprinkle with a little more dill and serve.

Serves 2.

SOLE FLORENTINE

3 TBSP. DRY WHITE WINE	2 Tbsp. Butter or Margarine
2 Lbs. Fillet of Sole	2 Cups Water
1 Can Cream of Shrimp Soup	2 Tbsp. Dried Bread Crumbs
2 Pkg. Frozen Chopped Spinach	2 Tbsp. Grated Parmesan
Salt	Cheese

Bring water to boil. Add 1 teaspoon salt. Simmer sole in water 10 minutes. Remove from water. Cook spinach and drain.

Heat soup to boiling, add wine, spread spinach on bottom of an oven proof platter, top with fish, then the soup. Combine butter, bread crumbs and cheese, sprinkle on top.

Place under broiler until delicately browned and heated.

Serves 6.

SALMON RIVER STEAK SURPRISE

1/4 CUP DRY WHITE WINE
2 Thick Salmon Steaks (1 Lb.)
Several Broken Up Bay Leaves
2 Thin Slices of Onion

Pinch of Nutmeg
Juice & Peel of 1 Lemon, Grated
2 Tbsp. Butter
Salt & Pepper to Taste

Preheat oven to 475 degrees.

Spray a shallow non-stick baking dish liberally with cooking spray. Arrange the onion slices on the bottom, along with the bay leaves, lemon |uice and peel, pinch of nutmeg.

Place salmon steaks on top. Spread lightly with soft butter or margarine and pour on the white wine.

Sprinkle with salt and pepper.

Bake uncovered 8 to 10 minutes, depending on thickness; don't overcook.

Remove bay leaves before serving.

Serves 2.

WINE QUIZ QUESTION 6

Which wine is driest?

A) Rose
B) Rhine
C) Chablis
D) Burgundy

SEAFOOD RISOTTO

1/2 CUP CHARDONNAY	10 Leaves Fresh Basil, Coarsely
8 Oz. Med. Shrimp, Cleaned	Chopped
16 Oz. Bay Scallops	1/2 Cup Heavy Cream
2 Tbsp. Garlic, Finely Minced	2 Tsp. Olive Oil

Fifteen minutes before preparing Risotto, prepare the seafood mixture.

Pour olive oil into a heavy skillet. Heat until hot and saute 1/2 of shrimp and scallop mixture until shrimp turns pink and feels firm.

Remove mixture with a slotted spoon.

Place remaining seafood in same skillet and cook as above.

Add chopped garlic to the dripping in the skillet and saute gently - do not overcook.

Add wine and deglaze all brown bits on bottom and sides of skillet.

Reduce liquid until syrupy and add warmed cream. Bring to a boil, stirring constantly, then lower heat.

Return seafood to skillet and toss well in the cream. Set aside.

In a 2 to 3 quart saucepan, boil 2 cups water and 1/2 tsp. salt.

Stir in 1 cup long grain white rice, not instant.

Cover tightly, lower heat and simmer for 20 minutes or until all water is absorbed.

Drain any extra water that may be in pan.

Place rice on a platter, top with warmed seafood and chopped basil and ground fresh black pepper.

Serves 4.

E-Z SOLE & SHRIMP

1 CUP WHITE WINE
4 Medium Size Fillets of Sole
1 Stick Butter
2 Cups Fresh Mushrooms, sliced
Salt and Pepper

½ lbs Cleaned Raw Shrimp, chopped
Seasoned Bread Crumbs
1 Lemon thinly sliced

In frying pan, sauté mushrooms and butter until mushrooms are tender and slightly browned. Keep warm and set aside.

Place fillets on wax paper and spread chopped shrimp onto sole.

Generously sprinkle with bread crumbs.

Roll fillets up and place in microwave safe dish in single layer.

Do not stack fish.

Add salt and pepper to taste.

Pour wine over fish and add more salt if necessary.

Cover fish with lemon slices and cover dish.

Place in microwave and cook on medium heat for 15 to 20 minutes. Times vary according to microwave.

Check fish after 15 minutes. Center should be white and flaky when stuck with fork. Shrimp should be pink.

Remove sole from oven and pour hot mushrooms and butter over dish. Serve immediately.

Serves 4.

Add salt to vegetables when cooking.

Mushrooms can be substituted with sautéed fresh spinach or broccoli for variation.

GARLIC SHRIMP MARSALA OVER LINGUINE

1/2 CUP DRY MARSALA	2 Tbs. Flour
1 lb Shrimp, peeled and deveined	1 Cup low sodium Chicken Broth
3 Cloves Garlic, finely minced	½ Cup Italian Parsley
1 Small Onion, finely chopped	Salt and Pepper
3 Tbs. Olive Oil	1 lb. Linquine

In large skillet add olive oil and heat. Do not burn. Add garlic and stir for 30 seconds. Add sliced onions and cook until transparent and tender, stirring occasionally. Keep heat at medium.

Add flour to mixture and stir until completely dissolved. Pour in wine with chopped parsley and bring to boil for a couple of minutes stirring constantly. Lower heat to medium and add shrimp. Cook until shrimp are lightly pink and tender.

Cook linguine in large pot boiling water with 1 tsp salt added for 12 minutes. (10 minutes for a firmer pasta.) Drain.

Place pasta in large serving dish and pour shrimp sauce over top.

Place some chopped parsley on top and serve.

Serves about 4 people.

WINE QUIZ QUESTION 7

Which wine goes best with swiss cheese?

A) Dry White
B) Fruity Red
C) Sturdy Rose
D) Cheap Chablis

SPIRITED VEGGIE LOVERS SAUTE

1 1/3 Cups Dry WHITE WINE
1 Small Eggplant, peeled and sliced thin
2 Fresh Red and/or Green Peppers, sliced
1 Small Red Onion, thinly sliced
1 Cup Broccoli Florets
1 Cup Sun Dried Tomatoes (2 fresh tomatoes cut in chunks can be substituted)
1 Cup Sliced Fresh Mushrooms
4 Cups Fresh, Washed Spinach or Baby Spinach with stems removed
Olive Oil
2 to 3 Cloves of Garlic, chopped
Salt and Pepper to taste

Lightly cover bottom of large skillet with olive oil. Oil must be hot but not smoking. Add all vegetables except spinach to pan. Add salt to taste.

Cook vegetables in oil on medium heat until vegetables are tender. If softer vegetables are preferred, cook longer.

Add garlic and continue cooking until garlic is slightly browned. Place raw spinach on top of vegetables and sprinkle a bit more salt on top. Using thongs, stir mixture until spinach is soft.

Add wine and cook on high heat, mixing ingredients together until wine is reduced slightly. More salt can be added if needed.

When all vegetables are cooked, add 1 lb of pasta (any favorite will work) to skillet and mix with vegetables.

Parmesan cheese can be generously sprinkled over top. Also Italian red pepper flakes can be added.

Serves 4 to 6 people.

This dish can also be used as a filling for burritos. Just sprinkle a little olive oil over warmed burrito, add generous amount of vegetables and wrap.

MUSHROOM LOVERS' PRONTO SPAGHETTI SAUCE

2 TBSP. DRY WHITE WINE
8 Oz. Can Tomato Sauce
4 Oz. Can Mushroom Stems
and Pieces, undrained

1/4 Tsp. Mixed Dried Herbs
1 Heaping Tsp. Garlic Powder
1 Tsp. Minced Fresh Onion

Combine Ingredients in saucepan, simmer, uncovered stirring occasionally, until sauce thickens, about 5 to 8 minutes.

Serves 2.

VINO CON CARNE

2 CUPS RED WINE
2 1/4 Tbsp. Olive Oil
2 Onions, Sliced
3 Cloves Garlic, Minced
1 1/2 Lbs Ground Chuck
1/2 Lb. Ground Pork
1 Chili Pepper, Cleaned
and Chopped

1 Heaping Tbsp. Flour
1/2 Tsp. Oregano
1/8 Tsp. Cayenne Pepper
1/8 Tsp. Paprika
1/2 Tsp. Cilantro
1 Can Red Kidney Beans
Salt and Pepper to Taste

In large saucepan, heat olive oil. Place sliced onion and chili pepper in oil and saute until onion is transparent. Add garlic and saute for 1 minute.

Add meat and saute until brown. Pour wine into pan and bring to boil.

Dissolve flour in small amount of water and add to wine. Add the remaining seasonings and stir. Simmer slowly until meat is tender for one hour.

Add kidney beans and cook for 5 minutes.

Serves 6 or more.

VERY BERRY JELLY

2 CUPS SWEET WHITE WINE   Juice of 1/2 Lemon
4 Cups Fresh Strawberries   1 Envelope unflavored Gelatin
1/2 Cup Sugar

Clean strawberries and cut in half. Place in large glass serving dish. Add lemon juice.

In small saucepan heat wine and sugar gently being careful not to boil.

Dissolve gelatin in small amount of water and add to wine. Remove from heat and stir occasionally until wine is cool. Pour over the strawberries and refrigerate until gelatin sets.

Garnish with whole strawberries which were set aside before.

Serves 4 to 6.

GASTON AVENUE TRIFLE

2 TABLESPOONS WINE   1 to 2 Cups Sweetened Fruit
Sponge or Layer Cake   1 Pkg. Vanilla Custard
1/2 Cup Jam or Jelly   1 Cup Whipping Cream

Place rounds of yellow sponge or layer cake in a deep dish.

Sprinkle cake with two tablespoons of wine.

Spread a half cup jam or jelly, or one to two cups sweetened fruit over cake pieces.

Prepare one package vanilla custard and cool, then pour over the cake.

Whip one cup whipping cream until stiff, then garnish cake with cream and some fresh fruit.

ANSWERS TO WINE QUIZ

1) C - Noah

2) A - Body

3) D - Any of the Above

4) D - Drink a Lot

5) A - Sugar

6) C - Chablis

7) A - Dry White

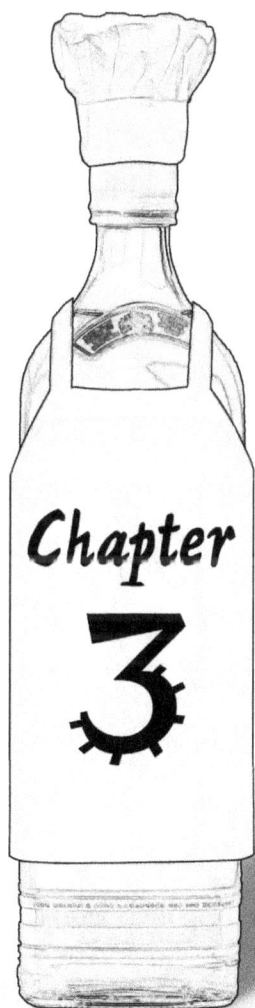

Variety and Whimsy with VODKA and WHISKEY

Chapter 3

Combine a hearty appetite with a devil-may-care mood and you're ready for cooking with VODKA and WHISKEY!

Though not traditionally used in cooking, pure and natural liquors can surprisingly bring out distinctive flavors of ingredients, much like cream or butter. This is true not only of VODKA and WHISKEY (also spelled "whisky") but also of their cousins, RYE and BOURBON.

BLOODY MARY SOUP

5 TBSP. VODKA	1 Tbsp. Sugar
1 1/2 Tbsp. Butter or Margarine	5 Cups Tomato Juice
1 Medium Onion, finely chopped	2 Tsp. Salt
2 Stalks Celery, diced	1 1/2 Tsp. Worcestershire Sauce
2 Tbsp. Tomato Puree	1 Tsp. Fresh Lemon Juice

In large saucepan, melt butter.

Add onion and celery and saute gently until softened.

Add puree, sugar and tomato juice.

Bring to boil, lower heat and simmer for 15 minutes, uncovered.

Add remaining ingredients.

Cool. Strain soup so that it has a smooth consistency.

Can be reheated or served cold.

Serves 6.

VODKA IN MELONS

Use a pastry syringe, like that used to put cream into cream puffs, to inject vodka into watermelon or a melon of your choice.

Place melon in refrigerator until quite cold.

Just before serving, cut melon into slices removing all seeds.

Serve on dessert plates and garnish with fresh mint.

This is a unique method of flavoring food from the inside out!

For vodka quantities see the introduction to chapter 7.

NEW YORK PORK TERRINE

3 TBSP. VODKA	Salt & Pepper to Taste
1/2 Lb. Chicken Liver	2 Cloves Crushed Garlic
3/4 Lb. Virginia Ham	2 Strips Bacon

Preheat oven to 400 degrees.

Grind liver and ham together. Add the seasoning garlic and vodka. Mix well. Pack mixture into a pint terrine or any small suitable oven-proof bowl.

Cut bacon into small squares and press into the mixture.

Cover and bake for 1 hour. Remove cover and bake for an additional 10 minutes.

Serves 4 to 6.

FILLET OF VEAL IN KUMQUAT AND VODKA SAUCE

2 TBSP. VODKA	3 Tbsp. Corn Oil
1 Lb. Veal Fillets	Juice of One Orange
Salt	1/2 Tsp. Ground Rose Pepper
Black Pepper	1 Tbsp. Parsley, minced
1/2 Cup Kumquats	1/2 Tsp. Salt
2 Tbsp. Sugar	

Place oil in skillet and lightly brown veal fillets. Roast in 400 degree oven for about 10 minutes until medium pink. Rub surface lightly with black pepper and salt. Allow to cool before slicing. To make marinade, rinse kumquats thoroughly and slice, removing seeds. Simmer in a saucepan containing sugar and 1 cup water until soft. Allow to cool then add vodka and remainder of ingredients. Slice fillet thin and spoon marinade over both sides of slices. Allow to marinate 1 hour before serving.

Serves 4.

VODKA QUIZ QUESTION 1

To drink Vodka "neat" means
to drink it...

A) From a mug
B) Through a straw
C) Without spilling
D) Not mixed

LOX-STYLE WHITEFISH
WITH BEET AND VODKA SAUCE

1 Smoked Whiteftsh
1 Tbsp. Salt
1 Tsp. Sugar

1 Tsp. White Pepper, ground
2 Tsp. Ground Dried Dill

SAUCE

2 TBSP. VODKA
2 Tbsp. Mustard
1 Tsp. Powdered Sugar

1 Tsp. White Vinegar
1 Tbsp. Vegetable Oil
1 Tsp. Juice from Canned Beets

Remove skin from fish. Cut in half and separate spine from fillet. Only use the fillets.   Place fillets in bowl and cover with salt, sugar, white pepper and dill and allow to season in refrigerator overnight.

To prepare sauce, mix mustard, powdered sugar and dash of vinegar in mixing bowl. Add oil a drop at a time beating vigorously. Add remainder of vinegar. Season with beet |uice and vodka. To serve, remove excess salt from fillet, place on plate, drench in sauce.

Serves 4.

PIKE IN VODKA TOMATO SAUCE

4 TBSP. VODKA

1 Lb. Pike Fillets,
    Skinned and Boned

2 Tsp. Salt

1 Tbsp. Dried Cilantro

1/2 Tsp. Black Pepper

1 Lb. Plum Tomatoes

1 Shallot, Chopped

1/2 Cup Tomato Juice

4 Drops Worcestershire

6 Drops Tabasco Sauce

1 Tbsp. Virgin Olive Oil

Cut tomatoes into chunks. Place in large saucepan and cook slowly until soft.

In large skillet heat oil and saute shallot. Add salt, cilantro, pepper, tomato juice, Worcestershire sauce, and Tabasco sauce.

Slowly simmer for about 20 minutes uncovered.

Add pike fillets and cover. Continue cooking on low heat until pike is white and flakes gently.

Serves 3.

AL'S VODKA FISH DISH

3 TBSP. VODKA

4 Thin Slices Smoked Salmon

1 Tsp. Salt

1 Tsp. White Pepper

Juice of One Lemon

2 Tbsp. Olive Oil

2 Tbsp. Chopped Fresh Dill

Coat salmon slices with salt and pepper.

Mix vodka and lemon juice and pour over salmon. Marinate for 1 hour then add olive oil.

Garnish with dill. Can be served with a mild vinaigrette sauce or tartar sauce.

Serves 3.

HERRING TARTARE AND MUSHROOMS IN BRINE

2 TBSP. VODKA
6 Herring Fillets
1 Medium Onion, Chopped
4 Tbsp. Capers
Chives or Leeks

4 Tbsp. Chopped Dill Pickle
4 Tbsp. Sour Cream
1 Small Jar Whole Mushrooms
   in Brine

Dice herring fillets and combine with remaining ingredients except mushrooms.

Drain mushrooms and chop. Spread mushrooms on plate and sprinkle generously with chives or leek.

Form herring mixture into serving size balls and place on mushrooms.

Serve with crackers or toasted bread slices.

Serves 4.

VODKA QUIZ QUESTION 2

What is vodka called in Poland?

A) Vodski
B) Wodka
C) Pivo
D) Dubzhe

BROILED SHELLFISH TARTARE

3 TBSP. VODKA
1/2 Cup Medium Whole Shrimp
1/2 Cup Diced Scallops
1/2 Cup Diced Cod
1 Small Onion, Diced
1 Leek, Diced

3 Tbsp. Anise Liqueur
Salt and Pepper
1 Cup Sour Cream
1/2 Cup Dried Bread Crumbs
1 Green Bell Pepper, Diced
1 Medium Egg

Combine fish, onion, leek, green pepper and egg.

Add salt and pepper to taste.

Shape into 4 patties.

Broil slightly on both sides. Do not overcook.

Combine sour cream, liqueur and vodka.

Serve patties on platter lengthwise. Pour sour cream sauce down center.

Garnish with thinly sliced strips of leek tops.

Serves 4.

GRILLED SOLE WITH HERBS AND BUTTER SAUCE

2 TBSP. VODKA
2 Shallots, minced
1 Tbsp. White Wine Vinegar
1/4 Lb. Sweet Butter
1/2 Pint Heavy Cream
1/2 Cup Mayonnaise
2 Sole Fillets, Halved

Lemon Juice
1 Tsp. Dried Basil
9 Whole Chives
1/4 Cup Italian Parsley, Fresh
1/2 Tsp. Salt
1 Clove Garlic, Crushed
1 Cup White Wine

Cooking insturctions on next page.

To prepare butter sauce, place shallots in saucepan with vinegar and wine and simmer reducing to 6 to 8 tablespoons. Remove from heat and add cubes of chilled butter, whisking constantly.

Shallots may be left in sauce or strained out.

Beat cream until stiff. Fold into sauce.

Season with salt, pepper and lemon juice. Place spices and vodka in blender and blend until smooth.

Add mayonnaise and continue blending. Mixture should have a creamy texture and a slight tinge of green color.

Oil bottom and sides of shallow baking dish. Place fillets in dish and spoon herb mayonnaise over them.

Bake in 400 degree preheated oven for 10 minutes or until fish flakes gently.

Serve with butter sauce and fresh vegetables.

Serves 4.

WHITE CHOCOLATE SNOWBALL

4 TBSP. VODKA	2 Tbsp. Green Peppercorns
1 Pint Half and Half	2 Tbsp. White Wine
6 Egg Yolks	5 Oz. White Chocolate
3/4 Cup Sugar	

To make ice cream, mix half and half, egg yolks and sugar in double boiler until thickened.

Chill custard slightly.

Simmer green pepper corns in white wine until soft. Stir crumbled white chocolate, vodka and peppercorns into custard and chill. Process in ice cream machine or whisk and freeze for 10 minutes repeating this process 10 times.

See TRUFFLE ICING *and* SAUCE FOR SNOWBALL *on next page.*

TRUFFLE ICING

2 Tbsp. Cocoa Liqueur   **2 Oz. Sweet Butter**
7 Oz. Dark Chocolate

To make truffle, heat liqueur to simmer in saucepan.

Beat in dark chocolate and butter. Chill.

SAUCE FOR SNOWBALL

Puree 1 pint fresh raspberries in small amount of water and 2 tablespoons sugar.

To create snowball, form ice cream into one large ball.

Frost with truffle icing and chill.

To serve, spoon raspberry sauce onto 4 plates. Cut ice ball into 4 slices and place over sauce.

Garnish with whole fresh raspberries.

Serves 4.

VODKA QUIZ QUESTION 3

How strong is the strongest vodka?

A) 100 Proof
B) 125 Proof
C) 160 Proof
D) 199.9 Proof

HAPPY HAZELNUT CAKE

3 TBSP. VODKA
8 Oz. Butter
1/4 Cup Sugar
2 Medium Eggs
1 Cup All Purpose Flour

2 Tsp. Baking Powder
1/2 Tsp. Cinnamon
1/2 Cup Hazelnuts, Chopped
2 Tbsp. Lemon Juice

Preheat oven 225 degrees.

Combine butter and sugar. Beat in eggs one at a time.

Mix dry ingredients and add to batter.

Stir in lemon juice, vodka and hazelnuts. Pour into greased 9 inch cake pan.

Bake for 45 minutes or until center is firm to touch.

Cool for 10 minutes and remove from pan.

ICING

4 Oz. Powdered Sugar
2 Oz. Butter, Softened
4 Oz. Unsweetened Chocolate

2 Tsp. Strong Coffee
2 Tsp. Vodka

Mix powdered sugar into butter.

Melt chocolate in double boiler, adding coffee.

Pour chocolate slowly into butter mixture.

Stir in vodka.

If icing seems too thick, add more vodka.

Spread icing on cool cake and garnish with chopped hazelnuts.

STRAWBERRY INTOXICATION

4 TBSP. VODKA
1 Pint Heavy Cream
3/4 Cup Sugar

4 Egg Yolks
1 Cup Pureed Strawberries

Heat cream, sugar and egg yolks in double boiler for about 30 minutes stirring constantly.

Pour mixture into chilled container immersing in ice to chill faster. Stir while cooling.

Fold in puree.

Check sweetness and stir in more sugar if necessary.

Place mixture in terrine and freeze overnight.

To serve, slice onto plates and allow to sit briefly until serving.

Garnish with whole strawberries and chocolate slivers.

Serves 4.

CLASSIC GELATIN SHOTS

Prepare your favorite flavor of gelatin according to the instructions on the box substituting some of the water with vodka.

Pour gelatin into 1 inch paper cups, place on tray and refrigerate.

To judge vodka quantity, see the introduction to Chapter 7.

Great for informal parties.

VODKA DESSERT SHAKE

1 CUP VODKA   1/2 Cup Sugar
1 1/4 Cups Frozen Strawberries Juice of 1 Orange
3 Tbsp. Fresh Basil, Minced   1 Tbsp. Lemon Juice
1/2 Cup Water   1 Cup Heavy Cream

Combine sugar and water by simmering slowly until sugar is melted. Do not boil.

Place all ingredients except cream in bowl and refrigerate for 1 hour.

Add heavy cream and thoroughly blend in processor.

Serve chilled in glasses.

Serves 4.

VODKA SUNDAE SUPREME

Place 1 large scoop of coffee ice cream in a fluted dessert glass.
Pour 1 teaspoon of vodka over ice cream. Drizzle chocolate syrup over dessert and sprinkle chopped almonds liberally on top.
Garnish with several chocolate covered coffee beans.

VODKA QUIZ QUESTION 4

To what does the term "Vodka Belt" refer?

A) A region where Vodka is popular

B) An oversized shot

C) A punch in a drunken brawl

D) An accessory for a vodka suit

SCHNORRER'S WHISKEY SCHNITZEL

1/2 CUP WHISKEY
4 Veal Cutlets
9 Tbsp. Olive Oil
1 Heaping Tbsp. Flour
1 Heaping Tbsp. Butter
1 Cup Milk
2 Cups Flavored Bread Crumbs

4 Tbsp. Tomato Paste
1/4 Tsp. Dried Basil
1 Stalk Celery, Minced
1 Small Onion, Minced
Salt and Pepper to Taste
2 Eggs

To make a white sauce combine one tablespoon of flour to one tablespoon of butter.

Add milk and mix thoroughly.

Set aside.

In small bowl, lightly beat eggs.

Dip cutlets in eggs and then in bread crumbs.

In large skillet, heat oil.

Place breaded cutlets in skillet and brown on both sides.

Add whiskey, tomato paste, basil, celery, onion, and pepper to white sauce.

Place sauce in medium saucepan, mix ingredients thoroughly and heat to simmer for several minutes.

Place veal cutlets on serving plate.

Pour white sauce over the cutlets and garnish with Italian parsley and black olives (optional).

Serves 4.

WHISKEY FRUIT SALAD

1/2 CUP WHISKEY

1 1 Lb. Can Pineapple Chunks, Drained

1 1 Lb. Can Grapefruit Sections, Drained

1/2 Cup Maraschino Cherries, or Strawberries, Halved

1 Cup Mandarin Orange Sections

1 Cup Peaches, Cut Up

1/2 Cup Shredded Coconut

2/4 Cup Orange Marmalade

Combine pineapple chunks, grapefruit sections, orange sections, cherries, peaches and coconut.

Warm orange marmalade slightly, remove from heat and mix with whiskey.

Pour over fruit and mix well.

Serves 6 to 8.

EASY-DOES-IT MINCEMEAT

1/2 CUP WHISKEY

1 Large Can Pears

8 Tbsp. Mincemeat

Preheat oven to 400 degrees.

Drain half the juice from the pears. Pour into small saucepan and add 2 tablespoons of whiskey.

Set aside.

In a large shallow serving dish, place pears flat side up. In the center of each pear half, place a spoonful of mincemeat and a teaspoon of whiskey.

Just before serving, heat syrup and whisky until hot but not boiling.

Pour over pears and garnish with maraschino cherries.

WHISKEY MEATBALLS

1/4 CUP WHISKEY
1 lb. Ground Chuck
3/4 Cup Herb Seasoned Stuffing
1/4 Cup Chili Sauce

1 Egg, Slightly Beaten
1/4 Tsp. Salt
2 Tbsp. Butter or Margarine

Mix stuffing and salt into ground chuck. Combine egg, chili sauce and whiskey. Pour mixture into meat and mix well. Form into small balls. Melt butter in large skillet. Brown meatballs on all sides over medium heat. Lower heat, cover skillet and cook 5 minutes more or until center of meatball is cooked through. Excellent appetizer.

Serves 3 to 6 .

REAL BOSS BARBECUE SAUCE

1/2 CUP WHISKEY
1 Medium Onion, Finely Chopped
2 Slices bacon, Finely Chopped
1 Pint Ketchup

1/2 Cup Brown Sugar
1 Tsp. Salt
1/2 Tsp. Chili Powder
Juice of One Lemon

Lightly brown onion and bacon. Remove from heat. Add ketchup and whiskey. Stir and add remaining ingredients. Simmer slowly for 10 minutes.

WHISKEY QUIZ QUESTION 1

Whiskeys are usually distilled in....

A) Steel Vats
B) Pine Casks
C) Oak Barrels
D) Copper Kettles

WHISKEY HAM STEAK

1/2 CUP WHISKEY	1/2 Cup Apple Cider or Juice
2 Lb. Ham Steak	1 Tbsp. Brown Sugar
1 Tbsp. Flour	2 Tbsp. Dijon Mustard
2 Tbsp. Butter or Margarine	

Melt butter in large skillet. Add ham. Cook until tender and browned on both sides.

Remove to platter. Keep warm. Add flour to drippings in skillet. Mix.

Cook, stirring two to three minutes.

In separate bowl, mix remaining ingredients until well blended. Slowly pour into skillet, stirring continually. Cook until thickened.

Serve immediately with ham steak.

Serves 4 to 6.

BILLY BOB'S BARBECUE SAUCE

3/4 CUP WHISKEY	2 Tbsp. Fresh Garlic, minced
2 Cups Ketchup	1/4 Cup Brown Sugar
2 Tbsp. Fresh Chopped Onion	1/4 Cup Vinegar
1/2 Tsp. Red Pepper Sauce	

In a saucepan, combine all ingredients except whiskey.

Simmer for 5 minutes.

Remove from heat and stir in whiskey. Use as basting sauce for chicken or ribs.

Generously brush on sauce several times during last 15 minutes of cooking.

Makes about 9 cups.

WHISKEY COCK-A-DOODLE

1/2 CUP WHISKEY	Juice of 1 Small Lemon
3 Tbsp. Softened Butter	1 Tbsp. Vegetable Oil
1 Frying Chicken, Cut in Pieces	2/3 Cup Heavy Cream
1 1/2 Tbsp. Mustard	Salt and Pepper

Mix softened butter with mustard, lemon juice, salt and pepper.

Cover pieces of chicken with butter paste.

In deep large skillet, heat oil and brown chicken pieces thoroughly.

Cover and cook for 90 minutes or until chicken is not longer pink inside.

Pour whiskey over chicken and cook for 5 minutes over low heat.

Pour warmed cream into skillet and simmer slowly for 10 minutes. Do not boil.

Serves 4.

WHISKEY FLAVORED BUTTER

2 TABLESPOONS WHISKEY   1 Cup Butter

With mixer, beat 2 tablespoons whiskey with 1 cup of butter until well blended.

Serve with pancake syrup on hot pancakes.

Also delicious served with toast, muffins, rolls or biscuits.

WHISKEY SHRIMP A LA LULU

1/3 CUP WHISKEY	1 Lb. Extra Large Shrimp
1 Lb. Bow Tie Macaroni	2 Tomatoes, Peeled
3 Tbsp. Olive Oil	1/2 Cup White Wine
1 Small Onion, Chopped	1/3 Cup Heavy Cream
2 Cloves Garlic, Crushed	2 Tsp. Cornstarch

In large pot boil macaroni in water and 1 teaspoon of salt for 15 minutes.

Drain, mix in a small amount of oil and set aside, covered.

In large skillet heat oil. Saute onion until transparent. Add garlic and cook just until garlic starts to turn lightly brown.

Add shrimp and chopped tomatoes.

Salt and pepper to taste.

Warm half the whiskey in a small pot and add to shrimp.

Set aflame, shaking the pan. Remove shrimp from skillet and keep warm. Mix together the remaining whiskey, cream and cornstarch, and add to the sauce in skillet.

Bring to a gentle boil.

Taste and add more salt if necessary.

Place macaroni on large serving platter, top with shrimp and cover with sauce.

Sprinkle some Parmesan cheese and chopped fresh parsley on top if desired.

Serves 4 to 6.

UNCLE AL'S PANCAKE SYRUP

Meat 2 tablespoons of **WHISKEY** and **1 cup maple syrup.**
Serve with butter on hot pancakes.

ALMOND ICE CREAM TRUFFLE

1 CUP WHISKEY	1 13 Oz. Can Evaporated Milk
3 Cups Sliced Almonds	3 Cups Sugar
1/2 Gallon Vanilla Ice Cream	1 Tsp. Vanilla
1 Stick Butter	1/2 Tsp. Salt
5 Oz. Unsweetened Chocolate	1/3 Cup Light Corn Syrup

Toast almonds in a 350 degree oven for 15 minutes, until golden brown, stirring every 3 minutes.

Form ice cream into balls 1" diameter and roll them in almonds.

Refreeze.

In a double boiler at low to medium heat, melt butter and chocolate.

Add remaining ingredients and cook, stirring often, until mixture reaches 170 degrees (use candy thermometer).

Pour sauce on serving plates and let cool.

Place ice cream balls on top. Serve with fork and spoon.

Serves 12.

EGGS-CITING OMELET FILLING

1/4 CUP WHISKEY
2 Tbsp. Butter or Margarine
3/4 Cup Scallions
1/4 Cup Red Pepper, Chopped

1 Cup Sliced Mushrooms
2 Cups Monterey Jack Cheese,
Shredded

Melt butter in medium skillet.

Add scallions, pepper and mushrooms.

Cook briefly, keeping vegetables tender crisp.

Mix in whiskey and 1 cup cheese.

Cook, stirring, until cheese is melted.

Sprinkle remaining cheese on completed omelet.

Makes filling for 8 egg omelet.

GRILLED SHRIMP A L'ORANGE

MARINADE
1 Cup Pineapple Juice
Juice of 2 Fresh Limes
Fresh Dill
1/2 Tsp. Salt
1/4 Tsp. Pepper

SAUCE
1/2 CUP WHISKEY
2 Tbsps. Horseradish Sauce
3 Drops Tabasco
2 Cups Orange Marmalade

Place 1 lb. cleaned large shrimp in marinade and leave for at least 1 hour.

Alternate shrimp on skewers with chunks of fresh pineapple and onion. Grill until done.

Before serving, heat sauce and serve in bowl with shrimp skewers.

NORTH POLE WHISKEY CAKE

1/4 CUP WHISKEY	1 Cup + 1/4 Cup Granulated
9 Egg Whites	Sugar
1/4 Tsp. Salt	1 1/4 Cups Sifted Flour
1 1/2 Tsp. Cream of Tartar	4 Egg Yolks
2 Tsp. Pure Vanilla Extract	1/4 Cup Chopped Walnuts

In large bowl, beat egg whites, salt, cream of tartar and vanilla until soft peaks form.

Slowly add 1 cup sugar while continuing to beat. Fold in flour in 4 parts.

In separate bowl, beat yolks, whiskey and remaining 1/4 cup sugar until pale yellow.

Fold egg yolk mixture into egg whites and flour mixture.

Sprinkle nuts in bottom of ungreased 10 inch tube pan. Pour in batter.

Bake in preheated 375 degree oven for 35 minutes or until toothpick inserted comes out clean.

Cool on rack for 15 minutes.

Glaze in saucepan, combining 1/2 cup whiskey, 3 tablespoons butter, 3/4 cup sugar and 1/3 cup water.

Heat, stirring, just to dissolve sugar. Do not boil.

With fork, poke holes in the cake. Drizzle with half of glaze.

Cool cake additional 10 minutes.

To remaining glaze, mix in 1 cup confectioners sugar. Remove cake from pan.

Frost. Sprinkle with chopped nuts.

Serves 10 to 12.

BIG JOHN'S WHISKEY DELIGHT

1/2 CUP WHISKEY	1 1/4 Cups Boiling Water
1 1/4 Cups Fresh Apricots,	1 Pkg. Apricot Gelatin
Pitted	1 Cinnamon Stick
Juice of 1/2 Lemon	4 Cloves
1/4 Tsp. Ground Cinnamon	1/2 Cup Chopped Almonds
1 Heaping Tbsp. Sugar	

Halve apricots and soak in whiskey for 48 hours.

Place apricots in blender and puree. Stir in the cinnamon, lemon juice and sugar.

Place dry gelatin in bowl and add cloves and cinnamon stick. Pour the boiling water over gelatin. Stir until dissolved. Cool.

Strain the liquid into the apricot mixture and leave until it starts to set. Stir well.

Pour into individual cups or one large bowl.

Top with whipped cream and chopped almonds.

Serves 6.

WHISKEY QUIZ QUESTION 3

All Irish whiskeys are aged for at least....

A) 5 Years
B) 7 Years
C) 10 Years
D) 12 Years

SILLY WHISKEY SYLLABUB

1/4 CUP WHISKEY
2/3 Cup Uncooked Oatmeal
5 Tbsp. Honey

1 1/4 Cups Heavy Cream
1 Tsp. Lemon Juice

In 400 degree preheated oven roast oatmeal on cookie sheet until golden brown, shaking occasionally.

Whip the cream until stiff.

Mix together the honey, whiskey and lemon juice, and add to cream.

Continue beating until cream is very stiff.

Fold in half the oatmeal.

Spoon into dessert glasses and chill.

Sprinkle with the remaining oatmeal before serving.

Serves 6.

WHISKEY CREAM DELIGHT

1/4 CUP WHISKEY
1 Envelope Unflavored Gelatin
2/3 Cup Cold Water

2 1/2 Cups Heavy Cream
2 Tbsp. Honey

Dissolve gelatin in the water.

Whip the cream until fairly thick and gently add the honey and whiskey.

Fold the gelatin into the whiskey mixture. Keep folding until the mixture starts to set or it will separate.

Pour into individual serving dishes and chill.

Serves 8.

86

IN THE PINK SALAD

1/2 CUP WHISKEY
1 1/4 Cups Cranberry Juice
    Cocktail
1 3 Oz. Pkg. Cherry Gelatin
2 Tbsp. Lime or Lemon Juice
1/2 Cup Sugar

1 Cup Seedless Grapes, Halved
1/2 Cup Finely Chopped
    Celery
1/2 Cup Chopped Walnuts
1/2 Cup Pitted Canned Bing
    Cherries

Heat cranberry juice and stir in gelatin until dissolved.

Remove from heat and add whiskey, lemon juice and sugar. Chill until mixture begins to congeal. Fold in remaining ingredients. Chill in lightly oiled mold until firm. Unmold on lettuce.

Serves 10.

ORANGE ANISETTE BUNDT CAKE

2 TBS. VODKA
½ Cup Anisette
1 Orange Cake Mix
1 Pkg. Vanilla Instant Pudding

4 Lg. Eggs
½ Cup Pure Vegetable Oil
½ Cup Fresh Orange Juice

Preheat oven to 350 degrees. Spray generously 12 cup Bundt pan with cooking spray. In electric mixing bowl, add cake mix, orange juice, eggs, pudding mix, oil, anisette and vodka. Mix on slow speed until all ingredients are wet. Scrape bowl and beat at medium speed for 3 minutes until batter is smooth. Bake cake for 50 minutes or until knife inserted comes out clean. The cake should be light golden brown. Remove cake from oven and place on wire rack for 15 minutes. After running a knife around the cake and the center tube, invert it to remove from pan. Place it back on rack until cool. Glaze can be drizzled over cake at this time. To make glaze, sift 1 1/2 cups confectioners' sugar, add 2 tbs. orange juice, 2 tbs. Anisette and 1 tbs.of vodka. The icing should not be thick but slightly runny so that it can be drizzled over cake. If icing is too thick, add a bit more juice. If it is too thin, add a bit more sugar. Great served with espresso. Serves 10.

BOURBON BONBONS

1/3 CUP WHISKEY   ¼ Cup Light Corn Syrup
3 1/2 Cups Vanilla Wafers   ¾ Cups Walnuts, chopped
2 tbs. Unsweetened Cocoa Powder 6 oz. Semi Sweet Chocolate Chips
½ Cups Confectioners' Sugar   1 Tbs. Butter

Roll out vanilla wafers with rolling pin until wafers are completely mashed and free of any large pieces.

Combine remaining ingredients, except for chocolate chips and butter. Roll mixture into one-inch balls.

Place chocolate chips in small saucepan and add the butter.

On low heat, melt chocolate until complete smooth. Do not boil.

Dip cookie balls into melted chocolate and place on cookie tray.

Refrigerate and serve cold.

ONION SOUP WITH BOURBON

½ CUP BOURBON   2 qts. Low Sodium Beef Broth
5 Cups Sliced Red Onions   ¼ Tsp. Basil
3 Tbs. Butter   8 Slices Toasted French Bread
3 Tbs. All Purpose Flour   1 Cup Grated Swiss Cheese

In a large sauce pan , sauté sliced onions in butter until onions are tender and soft.

Stir in flour to form a paste. Slowly pour in bourbon until mixture is smooth and without lumps. Gradually pour in beef broth and add basil. Simmer soup for 30 to 40 minutes.

Fill small soup bowls or French soup bowls with soup ¾ full. Place slice of toasted French bread on top of soup and sprinkle with cheese. Place bowls in broiler until cheese is bubbly. You can also use a microwave oven to melt cheese.

Serve immediately. Makes 8 bowls of soup.

SPAGHETTI MARTINI

(Spicy Mexican Spaghetti Sauce)

4 OZ. VODKA
3 Tbs. Vermouth
3 Tbs. Butter
1 Tbs. Olive Oil
2 Shallots, minced
4 Cloves Garlic, minced
1 Jalapeno Pepper, chopped
2 Medium Tomatoes, Chopped
2 Tbs. Lime Juice
2 Tbs. Tomato Paste
½ tsp.Ground White Pepper
¼ Tsp. Whole Ground Coriander
1 Tsp. Salt
1 Red Bell Pepper, diced
1-1/2 cups Heavy Cream
1/3 cup Fresh, Finely Chopped Cilantro
2 Tbs. Minced Parsley
1 lb. Spaghetti
Black Olives ,6 Sprigs Fresh Cilantro and Crushed Red Pepper for garnish

Heat butter and oil over medium heat in large saucepan.

Add shallots and garlic. Saute for about 2 minutes. Add the jalapeno and sauté for 30 seconds. Add tomatoes, Vodka, vermouth, lime juice, tomato paste, white pepper, ground coriander and salt and raise heat to high to reduce liquid. Stir often for about 3 minutes. Add the bell pepper and continue to simmer for until all ingredients are softened, about ½ hour. Do not cover.

Slowly add cream and reduce for about 10 minutes. The mixture should be a bit thickened and creamy. Just before sauce is done, add fresh cilantro and parsley.

Cook spaghetti in boiling water with 1 tsp. of salt.

Drain pasta thoroughly and place in serving dish.

Pour sauce over pasta.

Top with black sliced black olives and a sprig of fresh cilantro.

Sprinkle with crushed red pepper flakes for added heat. (Optional)

Serves 4.

WHISKEY QUIZ QUESTION 4

Who invented Whiskey?

A) Monks
B) Vikings
C) Cannibals
D) Cowboys

ANSWERS TO VODKA QUIZ

1) D - Not mixed
2) B - Wodka
3) C - 160 Proof
4) A - A region

ANSWERS TO WHISKEY QUIZ

1) C - Oak Barrels
2) C - Water of Life
3) B - 7 Years
4) A - Monks

Spirited Dishes from
TEQUILA & RUM

Chapter 4

TEQUILA & RUM are fiery liquors that are immensely popular in various cocktails but as a rule are not considered as culinary ingredients. But like many "rules", this one can be broken any time the cook feels adventurous and usually with excellent results! Rum cake, for example, is recognized as a classic dessert.

RODNEY'S RUM OMELET

1/4 CUP RUM	1/4 Tsp. Salt
4 Eggs	2 Tbsp. Dark Jam
1 Tbsp. Sugar	Sugar for Garnish

Separate the eggs. Stir the yolks with the sugar, beat the whites with the salt until stiff and fold into the yolk mixture.

Cook the omelet and fill with warmed jam.

Fold over, slide onto baking dish, and sprinkle with sugar.

Place omelet under a hot grill for a second or two.

Meanwhile warm the rum, pour it over the omelet, set alight and eat immediately.

Serves 2.

PDQ BBQ SAUCE

1 1/2 CUPS SPICED RUM	1/2 cup Chopped Onion
3/4 Cup Ketchup	1 Clove Garlic, Crushed
2 Tbsps. Cider Vinegar	1 Tsp. Prepared Mustard
1 Tbsp. Worcestershire Sauce	1/2 Tsp. Black Pepper
1 Tbsp. Brown Sugar	1/2 Tsp. Salt

Combine all ingredients in saucepan and mix well.

Bring to boil over medium heat.

Reduce heat and simmer for 15 minutes.

For chicken, beef or pork.

Makes 1 cup.

SPICED GRILLED SHRIMP

1/4 CUP SPICED RUM
2 Lbs. Large Fresh Shrimp
1 Cup Olive Oil
1 Tsp. Salt

1/2 Tsp. Tabasco
2 Cloves Garlic, Mashed
1/2 Cup Chili Sauce

Shell and devein shrimp. Leave tail shell attached.

Mix with remaining ingredients.

Marinate for 1 hour.

Thread onto skewers and place on grill 6 inches above gray coals.

Grill 2 to 3 minutes each side and baste often with marinade.

8 Appetizer Servings.

KILLER FRUIT KABOBS

1 TBSP. SPICED RUM
4 Large Firm Nectarines
1/4 Cup Fresh Lemon Juice

4 Tbsp. Butter
Vanilla Ice Cream

Cut each nectarine into 6 wedges and toss with lemon juice.

Place butter and rum in a small saucepan. Warm on edge of grill.

Thread nectarines on skewers and grill over a medium to low fire. Turn once and baste until browned outside but not too soft, about 10 minutes.

Serve warm from the grill on top of vanilla ice cream.

Serves 4.

PEPPY PINA COLADA DRESSING

DRESSING

1/4 CUP LIGHT RUM
1 Cup Heavy Cream
1/4 Cup Banana Yogurt

1/4 Cup Pineapple Juice
1 Tbsp. Coconut Cream

In medium bowl whip cream until thickened but not stiff.

Fold in yogurt, pineapple |uice, rum and coconut cream.

Makes approximately 1 and 3/4 Cups.

FRUIT SALAD

Arrange lettuce leaves on large platter.

Decoratively place desired fresh fruit, peeled and sliced, over lettuce.

Sprinkle with shredded coconut.

Serve with dressing.

MARVELOUS MARINADE FOR CHICKEN

1/2 CUP DARK RUM
2 Cups Fresh Orange Juice
Zest from Two Oranges
2 Tbsp. Chopped Mint
Curry Powder

Chopped Cilantro
Minced Garlic
1/4 Cup Soy Sauce
1 Whole Cut Up Chicken

Combine all ingredients in a shallow dish.

Place chicken in marinade overnight.

Grill chicken, basting with marinade until done.

BAKED APPLE
RUM JAM JUMBLE

1/2 CUP RUM   6 Large Apples
6 Tbsp. Apricot Jam   Butter
12 Tbsp. Raisins   Nutmeg

Peel and core apples and place in buttered baking dish.

Mix jam, raisins and nutmeg together. Spoon apricot mixture into center of apples. Drop a small piece of butter on top of each apple. Gently pour rum over top. Bake in preheated 400 degree oven for 20 minutes or until apples are tender. Can be served with heavy cream drizzled over top.

Serves 6.

RUM QUIZ QUESTION 1

Rum is distilled from....
A) Sugar Cane
B) Cane Sugar
C) Molasses
D) All of the Above

RUMMY RAISIN ICE CREAM

2 TBSP. RUM   1 Cup Raisins
1 Quart Vanilla Ice Cream

Melt ice cream slightly and mix in all ingredients. Place in bowl and freeze. To serve, place scoop of ice cream on small dessert plate. Sprinkle with several raisins which have been soaked in rum.
Serves 6.

BOMBAY LEMON SORBET

2 TBSP. RUM
3/4 Cup Sugar
1 1/4 Cups Water

Juice of Two Large Lemons
1 Egg White, Stiffly Beaten

Heat the sugar and water gently until the sugar melts.

Continue cooking for another 10 minutes. Cool.

When cold stir in fruit juice and strain into a bowl.

Place in freezer until mixture is almost frozen.

Place into another bowl, stir in the rum and fold in the egg. Freeze.

Serves 4.

VEGAS GINGER MELON

1/4 CUP RUM
1 Cantaloupe
1 1/2 Tsp. Powered Ginger

1/2 Cup Sugar
1 1/4 Cups Heavy Cream,
  Whipped

Cut melon in half and scoop out the seeds. Remove flesh while keeping shell intact.

Dice melon or shape into balls.

Place the melon pieces in a bowl with the ginger and sugar. Cover and chill.

Before serving, add the rum.

Return melon to shell halves. Serve with whipped cream.

Serves 4 to 6.

3 JIGGER STRAWBERRY CREAM

1 JIGGER LIGHT RUM
1 Jigger Cherry Liqueur
1 Jigger Orange Liqueur
6 Cups Fresh Strawberries

1/4 Cup Sugar
1 1/4 Cups Heavy Cream
1 Quart Strawberrry Ice Cream,
Slightly Soft

Clean strawberries and crush them slightly in serving bowl.

Add liqueurs.

Whip the cream and mix together with the ice cream.

Pour over strawberries and chill for 30 minutes.

Serves 8.

DAN'S RUM FLAN

1/4 CUP RUM
4 Oz. Semi-Sweet Chocolate
2 Cups Corn Flakes

1 1/2 Cups Finely Crumbled
Pound Cake
1 Pint Chocolate Ripple Ice Cream

Melt 3/4 of the chocolate in a non-stick pan.

Gently stir in corn flakes until they are evenly coated with chocolate.

Spread a 6 inch souffle dish with the mixture and chill.

Mix the crumbs with the rum and spread on top of corn flakes.

Spread the ice cream on top of this and decorate with remaining chocolate, grated.

Chill until ready to serve.

Serves 6.

DAIQUIRI PIE

1/2 CUP LIGHT RUM	2 Eggs, Slightly Beaten
1 Pkg. Lemon Instant Pudding	2 Cups Non-dairy Whipped
1 Pkg. Lime Flavor Gelatin	Topping, Thawed
1/3 Cup Sugar	1 Baked 9" Crumb Cracker Crust,
2 1/2 Cups Water	Cooled

Mix pudding, gelatin and sugar in saucepan.

Stir in 1/2 cup water and eggs. Blend well.

Add remaining water. Stir over medium heat until mixture comes to full boil.

Remove from heat and stir in rum.

Chill about 1 1/2 hours.

Blend whipped topping into cooled mixture. Spoon into crust.

Chill until firm, about 2 hours.

Garnish with additional whipped topping, lime or lemon slices or graham cracker crumbs.

RUM QUIZ QUESTION 2

What island is called "Rum Island"?

A) Puerto Rico
B) St. Croix
C) Jamaica
D) Staten Island

SUMPTUOUS PEACH COBBLER

1/2 CUP LIGHT RUM

6 Cups Peeled and Sliced
  Peaches
1/2 Cup Brown Sugar
2 Tbsp. Com Starch
1 Tbsp. Lemon Juice
2 Tsp. Butter
1 Cup Chopped Walnuts

STRUSSEL TOPPING
1 Cup Pancake Mix
1/2 Cup Rolled Oats
1/2 Cup Brown Sugar
4 Tbsp. Margarine
1/2 Tsp. Ground Cinnamon

Preheat oven to 375 degrees. In a large bowl, combine peaches, light rum, brown sugar, corn starch, lemon juice and walnuts. Place in a oven proof casserole dish. Dot with margarine. Set aside.

In a small bowl, combine all topping ingredients and working quickly with fingers, mix it until it resembles a course meal. Sprinkle over peaches and bake for 45 minutes. Serve warm and top with vanilla or rum raisin ice cream.

SATINY STRAWBERRY MOUSSE

1/2 CUP LIGHT RUM
10 Oz. Frozen Strawberries,
  thawed
1 Cup Sugar

2 Pkgs. Unflavored Gelatin
2 1/2 Cups Heavy Cream,
  divided
1/2 Cup Water

Soften gelatin in half a cup of water. Heat over low heat until gelatin is dissolved. Cool to room temperature.

Puree strawberries in blender or food processor. Add sugar and mix well. Add cooled gelatin and stir well. Place mixture in refrigerator until it starts to set.

Whip 1 1/4 cups of the cream and pour into a 2 quart souffle dish or serving bowl. Refrigerate. When firm, decorate with remaining cream, whipped, and fresh sliced strawberries.

Serves 4 to 6.

CLASSIC RUM BALLS

1/4 CUP DARK RUM
1 1/2 Cups Vanilla Wafer
   Crumbs

1/4 Cup Honey
2 Cups Ground Walnuts
Confectioners Sugar

In medium bowl, combine all ingredients except sugar. Shape into 1" balls.

Roll in sugar. Store in tightly covered container.

Makes 2 and 1/2 Dozen.

GOLDEN RUM CAKE

1/2 CUP DARK RUM
1 Pkg. Vanilla Instant Pudding
1/2 Cup Cold Water
1 Cup Chopped Walnuts

1 Pkg. Yellow Cake Mix
4 Eggs
1/2 Cup Vegetable Oil

Preheat oven 925 degrees.

Grease and flour 10" tube or 12 cup bundt pan. Sprinkle nuts over bottom of pan.

Place cake mix in mixing bowl. Add egg, water, oil and instant pudding. Blend ingredients on low for 2 minutes. Mix at medium speed for 4 minutes more.

Pour batter over nuts.   Bake 1 hour. Cool. Invert on cake plate and prick top. Spoon and brush glaze evenly over top and sides.

Allow cake to absorb glaze. Repeat until glaze is used up.

Glaze:

Melt 1/4 pound butter in saucepan. Stir in 1/4 cup water and 1 cup granulated sugar. Boil 5 minutes, stirring constantly. Remove from heat and stir in 1/2 cup rum.

DOUBLE CHOCOLATE RUM CAKE

1 CUP DARK RUM	4 Eggs
1 Pkg. Chocolate Cake Mix	12 Oz. Semi-Sweet Chocolate
1 Pkg. Chocolate Instant Pudding	1 Cup Raspberry Preserves
3/4 Cup Wafer	2 Tbsp. Shortening
1/2 Cup Vegetable Oil	1 Oz. White Chocolate

Preheat oven at 350 degrees. Combine cake mix, pudding, eggs, 1/2 cup rum, water and oil in large mixing bowl.
Using electric mixer, beat at low speed until moistened. Beat at medium speed for 2 minutes.

Stir in 1 cup of chocolate pieces. Pour batter into prepared greased 12 cup bundt or 10" tube pan.

Bake 50 to 60 minutes until cake tests done. Cool in pan for 15 minutes.

Remove from pan, cool on rack.

In small saucepan, heat raspberry preserves and remaining 1/2 cup rum.

Strain through sieve to remove seeds.

Place cake on serving plate. Prick surface of cake with fork. Brush raspberry glaze evenly over cake, allowing cake to absorb glaze. Repeat until all glaze has been absorbed.

In bowl, combine remaining 1 cup chocolate pieces and shortening. Microwave on high for 1 minute or until melted. Stir until smooth or melt mixture over hot (not boiling) water until chocolate is melted and mixture is smooth.

Spoon chocolate icing over cooled cake. Let stand 10 minutes.

In small bowl, combine white chocolate and 1 teaspoon of water.

Microwave on high for 30 seconds or until melted. A double boiler can be used instead.

Drizzle on top of chocolate icing.

YUM YUM RUM CAKE

Prepare your favorite yellow cake mix as directed on the package.

Turn the batter into a bundt pan or regular tube pan. Bake following package directions.

When cake is done, turn out on rack.

Heat **1/3 CUP RUM** with 3 tablespoons honey, spoon over hot cake.

Cool before serving.

RUM QUIZ QUESTION 3

The Daiquiri cocktail was named after a town in....

A) France

B) Japan

C) Brazil

D) Cuba

VIRGIN RUM SYRUP

In a small heavy bottomed saucepan, combined 1/2 cup each water and sugar.

Bring to boil over moderate heat and cook 1 minute without stirring.

Remove from heat. Cool slightly and stir in **1/2 CUP RUM**.

Makes about 1 and 1/2 cups.

Try it over fresh fruit!

BOOZY BANANA BREAD

1/2 CUP RUM	2 Cups Flour
1/2 Cup Butter, Softened	1 Tsp. Baking Soda
1 Cup Sugar	1 Tsp. Baking Powder
2 Eggs, Beaten	1/2 Tsp. Salt
3 to 4 Ripe Bananas, Mashed	1/2 Cup Chopped Nuts

Preheat oven to 350 degrees.

In large mixing bowl, cream butter, sugar and eggs.

In separate bowl, combine bananas and rum. Sift dry ingredients together except nuts. Gradually beat banana and flour mixtures into eggs. Stir in chopped nuts.

Turn into well greased loaf pan. Bake 1 hour.

Makes 1 loaf.

JAZZY GINGER COOKIES

1/2 CUP SPICED RUM	Pinch of Salt
1 Cup Sweet Butter, Softened	3 Tbsp. Crystallized Ginger,
1 Cup Confectioners Sugar	Minced
2 1/2 Cups Flour	1 Tsp. Ground Ginger

In large bowl, cream butter and sugar.

Add remaining ingredients. Mix until dough is workable. Shape dough into cylinder (2" diameter). Wrap in plastic and refrigerate 2 hours or freeze for 45 minutes.

Slice dough into rounds 1/4 inch thick. Place rounds on ungreased cookie pan about 2 inches apart. Bake at 400 degrees about 12 minutes or until edges are lightly browned.

Remove to rack.

Makes about 6 Dozen.

HOLIDAY HOOCH SQUARES

1/2 CUP RUM	1 Tsp. Vanilla
1 Cup Chopped Pitted Dates	1/2 Tsp. Salt
1 Cup Candied Fruit, Chopped	2/4 Cup Flour
1 Cup Golden Raisins	3/4 Tsp. Baking Powder
4 Eggs	1 Cup Walnuts, Chopped
1 Cup Sugar	

Marinate fruits in rum for up to 24 hours.

Grease and flour jelly roll pan (15 1/2" by 10 1/2"). In bowl, beat eggs and add sugar, vanilla and salt. Gradually stir in flour, baking powder, marinated fruits and nuts. Spread in pan and bake for 30 minutes at 350 degrees.

Cool and cut into squares.

Makes 32.

FEE-FI-FO-FUM RUM CAKE

Prepare 3 layers 9" yellow cake or sponge cake. Cool.

Split each into two. Prick layers with a fork and sprinkle with Virgin Rum Syrup (See recipe earlier in this chapter) to moisten.

In the top of a double boiler, melt together 1 stick butter and 8 oz. semi-sweet chocolate. Stir until smooth.

Remove from heat and add **1/2 CUP RUM**.

Beat in 1 stick softened butter alternately with 1 pound sifted confectioners sugar.

Frost 5 layers, setting one on top of the other. Place unfrosted layer on top.

Spread remaining frosting over top and sides and refrigerate an hour or longer, or freeze.

Makes about 8 servings.

ITALIAN RUM CAKE

3 EGGS   **2 Tsp. Vanilla Extract**

1 Cup Sugar   **1 Cup Sifted All-Purpose Flour**

3 Tbsp. Cold Water   **2 Tsp. Baking Powder**

Beat eggs until light. Gradually beat in the sugar. Keep on beating until mixture is thick and pale in color. If possible use an electric beater at high speed for 6 minutes.

Stir in water and vanilla.

Sift flour with baking powder. Fold into batter.

Bake in greased and floured 9" spring form pan in preheated 350 degree oven for 20 minutes or until cake tests clean.

Cool in pan while making the topping.

Pour topping over cooled cake in pan and chill until serving time.

To serve remove cake from pan and garnish with orange segments, maraschino cherries and rosettes of whipped cream.

Makes 6 to 8 servings.

Topping

Soften 1 envelope unflavored gelatin in 1/4 cup cold water. Stir in 2 cups hot milk and 3/4 cup sugar.

Cook over low heat until mixture is hot and gelatin is dissolved.

Mixture must not boil.

Gradually add 4 eggs yolks lightly beaten, stirring constantly.

Stir in **1/3 CUP DARK RUM.**

Set pan in bowl of cracked ice and stir constantly until mixture cools and begins to set.

Peel 1 orange and separate info segments. Fold orange segments and 1 cup heavy cream into custard.

NORWEGIAN RUM CREAM

1/4 CUP RUM	1 1/2 Tbsp. Unflavored Gelatin
2 Eggs, Separated	3 Tbsp. Cold Water
6 Tbsp. Sugar	2 Cups Heavy Cream, Whipped

Beat egg yolks and sugar together over very low heat until smooth and slightly thickened. Cool. Soak gelatin in cold water for 5 minutes.

Put gelatin over very low heat and stir until dissolved. Add to egg yolk mixture. Cool. Fold in whipped cream, rum and egg whites, beaten until stiff but not dry. Pour mixture into lightly oiled 1 1/2 quart mold. Chill until firm. Unmold and serve with sweetened berries or with small nut cookies.

Serves 6 to 8.

RUM LOVER'S BROWNIES

1/2 CUP RUM	1/2 Tsp. Salt
5 Ozs. Unsweetened Chocolate	2 Cups Sugar
2/3 Cup Butter	1 Tsp. Vanilla Extract
1 Tbsp. Instant Coffee	1/2 Cup Sifted All Purpose flour
5 Eggs	2 1/2 Cups Chopped Walnuts

In double boiler, melt chocolate and butter. When smooth, add instant coffee and set aside to cool.

Beat eggs and salt together until slightly fluffy. Add sugar gradually and beat until mixture is ribbony (about 10 minutes). Add vanilla extract, rum and cooled chocolate to eggs while beating on low speed. Fold in sifted flour until just incorporated, then fold in nuts. Pour batter on to greased, floured and parchment lined 11" by 17" baking pan.

Place in preheated 450 degree oven, lowing temperature to 375 degrees. Bake 20 to 22 minutes or until sides are dry and center is slightly soft. Do not over bake.

Makes 20 3" by 3" brownies.

CHEERY CHEESE CAKE TOPPING

1/4 CUP RUM

1 Cup Sugar

2 Tbsp. Corn Starch

1 Pint Fresh Strawberries, Sliced

1/4 Cup Orange Juice

1 Medium Orange, Pared and Cut Into Sections

1 Medium Banana, Diced

Combine sugar and cornstarch and mix well.

Crush 1 cup of the strawberries and add to sugar mixture along with orange juice and mix well.

Cook over medium heat, stirring constantly, until thickened and clear.

Chill.

Add fruits and mix lightly but thoroughly.

Spread mixture over the top of your favorite cheesecake.

Refrigerate 3 to 4 hours before serving.

RUM QUIZ QUESTION 4

Which of these is not a rum flavoring?

A) Mango

B) Mint

C) Licorice

D) Nougat

DOLORES' RAPTUROUS RUM CAKE

1/2 CUP DARK RUM
1 Cup Chopped Pecans
1 18 Oz. Pkg. Yellow Cake Mix
1 4 Oz. Pkg. Vanilla Instant Pudding

4 Eggs
1/2 Cup Cold Water
1/2 Cup Vegetable Oil

GLAZE
1/2 CUP DARK RUM
1/4 Lb. Butter

1/4 Cup Water
1 Cup Granulated Sugar

Preheat oven to 325 degrees. Grease and flour 10 inch tube. Sprinkle nuts over bottom of pan. Mix all cake ingredients together. Pour batter over nuts. Bake 1 hour. Cool.

Invert on serving plate. Prick top. Spoon and brush glaze evenly over top and sides. Allow cake to absorb glaze.

Glaze: Melt butter in saucepan. Stir in water and sugar. Boil 5 minutes, stirring constantly. Remove from heat. Stir in rum.

RANDY'S RUM NUTS

2 Tbs. Dark Rum
2 cups Walnut halves
¼ cup Sugar

2 Tsp Instant Coffee
¼ Tsp Cinnamon
1 Dash of Salt

Combine all ingredients in a small saucepan and cook over medium heat, stirring constantly for about 15 minutes, until sugar is well melted and nuts are completely coated.

Pour out onto wax paper, which has been sprayed with cooking spray.

Separate nuts as they cool.

Can be stored in covered glass jar or cookie can.

111

SHRIMP AMD PEPPER KABOBS

1/4 CUP TEQUILA
1/3 Cup Margarita Mix
1/4 Cup Canola or Vegetable Oil
2 Tbsp. Red Pepper Flakes
2 Lg. Cloves Garlic, Minced

24 Lg. Raw Shrimp, Peeled with
    Tails Intact
1 Each: Green, Red and Yellow
    Pepper, Cut into 1" Squares

Combine first 5 ingredients in shallow glass dish.

Add shrimp. Cover and refrigerate 1 hour.

Reserve tequila mixture.

Arrange shrimp and peppers on skewers. Grill or broil until shrimp turn pink.

Heat tequila mixture until boiling. Simmer 5 minutes. Serve with kabobs for dipping.

Makes 8 Kabobs.

TORTILLA PINWHEELS

1 3 Oz. Pkg. Cream Cheese,
    Softened
4 Oz. Can Green Chilies, Diced
1 Tbsp. Tequila
4 Flour Tortillas

4 Oz. Fresh Cooked Lobster,
    Chopped
1 Tbsp. Each: Fresh Cilantro,
    Onion, Chopped

Combine all ingredients, except tortillas.

Spread mixture on tortillas. Roll like a jelly roll. Wrap and chill.

Slice and serve.

Makes 48 rounds.

TEQUILA QUIZ QUESTION 1

Who invented tequila?

A) Don Juan

B) Vasco De Gama

C) Montezuma

D) Don Antonio De Cuervo

FIESTA GUACAMOLE

1 TBSP. TEQUILA

2 Ripe Avocados, Seeded and Chopped

3 Tbsp. Fresh Lime Juice

1 Sm. Tomato, Seeded and Chopped

2 Green Onions, Thinly Sliced (Include Green Top)

2 Tbsp. Fresh Cllantro, Chopped

1 Sm. Minced Jalapeno Pepper

Salt

1 Sm. Clove Garlic, Minced

With fork, coarsely mash avocados with lime juice.

Mix in remaining ingredients. Serve with tortilla chips for dipping.

Makes about 3 cups.

TEQUILA QUIZ QUESTION 2

What soft drink goes into a Tequila Fizz?

A) Cola

B) Club Soda

C) Ginger Ale

D) Cream Soda

CHICKEN TEQUILA SUNRISE

1/4 CUP TEQUILA
2 Lb. Cut-Up Frying Chicken
2 Onions, Thinly Sliced
3/4 Cup Orange Juice
1 Clove Garlic, Minced

2 Tsp. Dried Oregano
1 Tsp. Cumin Seeds (or 1/4 Tsp.
   Cumin Powder)
Salt and Coarsely Ground Pepper

Spray a shallow non-stick baking pan with cooking spray. Put the chicken pieces skin-side up, unseasoned in pan. Place pan in preheated 425 degree oven for 20 minutes, to crisp the skin and melt the fat.

Remove from oven and pour off all the fat. Put the onion slices under the chicken. Combine remaining ingredients and pour over the chicken.

Return to the oven for an additional 20 minutes or more until chicken is tender and crisp and liquid is reduced to a thick glaze. Baste frequently with pan liquid, adding a tablespoon of water if the liquid evaporates too much.

Serves 4.

ZELDA'S ZESTY CHICKEN WINGS

2 TBSP. TEQUILA
1/4 Cup Soy Sauce
1 Tbsp. Honey
1 Tbsp. Dijon Mustard

1 Clove Garlic, Crushed
1/4 Tsp. Hot Pepper Sauce
2 Lbs. Chicken Wings

In mixing bowl, combine first 6 ingredients.

Put chicken wings, cut in half, into large plastic bag. Pour in marinade and refrigerate for several hours.

Drain chicken and arrange on baking sheet. Bake at 450 degrees for 15 minutes. Reduce heat and bake for 20 minutes at 375 degrees.

Serve as an appetizer.

CHILE CHEESE SHRIMP

2 TBSP. TEQUILA
1 Lg. Onion
1 Lg. Clove Garlic, Minced
1 Tbsp. Olive Oil
1 Lg. Tomato, Coarsely Chopped
2 Fresh Jalapeno Chilles,
Chopped

1/8 Tsp. Cinnamon
2 Lbs. Shredded Cheese (Combo
of Mild Cheddar, Monterey Jack
and Munster)
1/2 Lb. Tiny Cooked Shrimp
1 10 Oz. Bag Tortilla Chips

Heat oven to 450 degrees.

Cook onion and garlic in oil in sauce pan until onion is soft. Mix in tomato, Chilles, Tequila and cinnamon.

Spread cheese In oven-proof serving dish. Spoon tomato mixture in center of cheese. Sprinkle with shrimp.

Bake 5 to 10 minutes or until cheese is melted.

Garnish with cinnamon sticks. Serve with tortilla chips.

Serves 8 to 10 as an appetizer.

TEQUILA QUIZ QUESTION 3

Tequila is named after a city in...

A) Argentina
B) Brazil
C) Mexico
D) Spain

CHEESE ENCHILADA ENCHANTMENT

2 TBSP. TEQUILA
1 16 Oz. Carton Cottage Cheese
3 Cups Cheddar Cheese, Shredded
1 1/2 Cups finely Chopped Green Onion
12 Corn Tortillas (6" Diameter)

1/2 Tsp. Dried Oregano
Salad Oil
2 (12 Oz. Jars) Thick Green Chili Salsa
1 Cup Shredded Lettuce
2 Med. Tomatoes, Thinly Sliced

Mix Tequila, cottage cheese, 1 cup cheddar cheese, onions and oregano. Set aside. Pour 1/4 inch oil into 10 inch frying pan on medium high heat. When oil is hot, cook each tortilla until limp and slightly blistered (about 10 seconds per side). Add oil when needed. Drain and place tortillas aside. Spread 1/3 cup cheese filling down center of each tortilla. Roll tortilla around filling. Place, seam side down, in baking dish. Cover with remaining green chili salsa and cheddar cheese. (May cover and refrigerate until next day.) Bake, uncovered, in preheated 350 degree oven for 20 minutes (30 minutes if refrigerated). Garnish with lettuce and tomatoes. Serves 6.

TEQUILA QUIZ QUESTION 4

What seasoning best accents tequila?

A) Salt
B) Pepper
C) Garlic
D) Paprika

SUZANNE'S VEGGIE CHILI

1/4 CUP TEQUILA
1 Lg. Onion, Chopped
2 Lg. Cloves Garlic, Minced
1 Tbsp. Olive Oil
2 Stalks Celery
2 Cans (7 Oz. Each) Sliced
   Green Chilies

1 Can (16 Oz.) Pinto or Gabanzo
   Beans
1/2 Tsp. Ground Cumin
2 Tsps. Chili Powder
1/2 Tsp. Hot Sauce
1 Can (12 Oz.) Whole Corn
Salt and Ground Pepper to Taste

In large skillet, cook onion and garlic in oil.

Stir in remaining ingredients except corn, tequila, salt and pepper. Simmer, until thickened. Add corn, tequila, salt and pepper.

Top with sour cream and shredded cheese.

Serves 4 to 6.

PORK CUBES WITH
RED PEPPER DIPPING SAUCE

1/4 CUP TEQUILA
1/2 Cup Margarita Mix
2 Tbsp. Brown Sugar
2 Lg. Cloves Garlic
1/4 Cup Sliced Green Onions
2 Lbs. Boneless Pork, Cut in 1 inch Cubes

1 Jar (9 Oz.) Roasted Peppers
1 Fresh Jalapeno Chili, Chopped
1 Lg. Clove Garlic
1 Small Onion, Chopped
1/4 Cup Olive Oil

Combine first 6 ingredients in large skillet.

Cook, uncovered, about 35 minutes or until pork is tender. While pork is cooking, combine remaining ingredients for sauce in processor. Blend until smooth .

Serve sauce for dipping pork cubes.

Serves 8.

ANSWERS TO TEQUILA QUIZ

1) D - Don Antonio DeCuervo
2) C - Ginger Ale
3) C - Mexico
4) A - Salt

ANSWERS TO RUM QUIZ

1) D - All of the Above
2) A - Puerto Rico
3) D - Cuba
4) C - Licorice

CORDIALS
in the
Kitchen

Chapter
5

CORDIALS as ingredients in cooking can be a surprising source of taste revelations.

A wide variety of food types react very favorably in the company of these versatile, flavorful liquors.

Please note - The terms "cordial" and "liqueur" are often used interchangeably. Although they have a great many similarities, one distinct difference is that liqueurs are usually flavored with herbs while cordials are generally created with fruit pulp or juices. However, since in reference to their products most producers of spirits predominately use the term "liqueur" in place of "cordial", the former is often used in this book to refer to either.

RICHARD'S ROAST TURKEY WITH CRANBERRY SAUCE

1/2 CUP CRANBERRY LIQUEUR	1/2 Cup Water
1/2 Cup Chopped Onion	1 Tbs. Chicken Broth
1/2 Cup Chopped Celery	1 Tsp. Sage
1/2 Lb. Sausage Meat, Cooked, Drained and Crumbled	1/2 Tsp. Each: Salt & Basil
	10 - 12 Lb. Turkey
1 Pkg. (8 Oz.) Herb Seasoned Stuffing Mix	Salt and Pepper to Taste
	Oil
1/2 Cup Chopped Pecans	1 Can (8 Oz.) Whole Cranberry Sauce

In large skillet, cook onion and celery in butter until soft. Mix in sausage, stuffing mix, cranberry sauce, pecans, liqueur, broth, sage, salt and basil.

Sprinkle turkey cavity with salt and pepper. Fill with stuffing mixture. Truss. Brush skin with oil. Place on rack in roasting pan.

Roast in preheated 325 degree oven for 3 1/2 4 hours or until tender.

Serve with Cordial Cranberry Sauce.

Serves 8 to 10.

CORDIAL CRANBERRY SAUCE

Combine 2 cups boiling water with 1 6 oz. package of raspberry flavored gelatin.

Stir several minutes or until dissolved. Mix in 3/4 cup **CRANBERRY LIQUEUR**, 1 16 oz. can whole berry cranberry sauce, 1 20 oz. can crushed pineapple, undrained and 1/4 cup chopped pecans.

Pour into 7 cup mold. Chill until firm. Unmold on serving platter.

Serves 8 to 10.

CRANBERRY CANDIED YAMS

1/2 CUP CRANBERRY
  LIQUEUR
1/2 Cup Butter or Margarine
2 Tbsp. Brown Sugar

1 Tsp. Orange Rind, Finely Grated
1 Can (24 Oz.) yams, drained
  and Sliced

In large skillet, melt butter with brown sugar, liqueur and orange rind.

Place potato slices in syrup. Simmer 3 to 4 minutes on each side or until well glazed.

Serves 4 to 6.

AWESOME ACORN SQUASH

1/2 CUP CRANBERRY
  LIQUEUR
3 Med. Acorn Squash, Halved

Salt
3 Tbsp. Butter or Margarine
8 Oz. Can Whole Cranberry
  Sauce

Place squash, cut side down, in shallow baking dish.

Bake in preheated 400 degree oven for 35 minutes.

Remove from oven and invert squash. Sprinkle salt. Place 1 teaspoon butter in each squash.

Combine liqueur and cranberry sauce. Spoon into squash cavity.

Return to oven. Continue baking for 30 minutes or until squash is tender.

Serves 6.

SUCCULENT SWEET AND SOUR PORK CHOPS

3/4 CUP CRANBERRY
 LIQUEUR
6 Center Cut Pork Chops,
 1" Thick, Trimmed
Salt & Pepper to Taste
1 Med. Onion, Sliced
1 Med. Clove Garlic, Minced
1 Small Green Pepper, Diced

1 Can (8 Oz.) Pineapple Chunks,
 Undrained
Juice of 1 Fresh Lemon
1 Tbsp. Soy Sauce
1 Pkg. (10 Oz.) Frozen Pea Pods
2 Tbsp. Sliced Pimentos
3 Tbsp. Cornstarch
3 Tbsp. Water

In large skillet, brown chops well on both sides. Sprinkle with salt and pepper.

Add onion, garlic, liqueur, pineapple, lemon juice, green pepper and soy sauce. Simmer 1 hour or until chops are tender. Blend into pan liquid.

Add pea pods and pimentos. Continue simmering for 5 minutes or until pea pods are tender crisp.

Serve on bed of rice.

Serves 4 to 6.

SAVORY BAKED CHICKEN

1/4 CUP CRANBERRY
 LIQUEUR
1/4 Cup Russian Salad Dressing

1 Envelope Onion Soup Mix
3 to 3 1/2 Lbs. Chicken Pieces

In medium bowl, mix salad dressing, liqueur and onion soup mix.

Dip each chicken piece in mixture to coat thoroughly. Place in 9" by 19" baking pan. Bake in preheated 350 degree oven 1 hour or until tender. Serve on bed of buttered noodles.

Serves 6.

PEACHY PORK LOIN

3/4 CUP PEACH SCHNAPPS   1/2 Tsp. Allspice
3 - 4 Lb. Boneless Pork Loin   1 Tsp. Salt
     Roast   2 Tbsp. Soy Sauce
2 Med. Cloves Garlic, Minced   2 Tbsp. Brown Sugar
1 Tsp. Freshly Ground Pepper   2 Tbsp. Dijon Mustard
1/2 Tsp. Cinnamon   1 Can (16 Oz.) sliced peaches,
1/2 Tsp. Cloves   Drained

Cut small slits in roast.

Combine garlic, pepper, cinnamon, cloves, allspice and salt. Rub into roast.

Refrigerate overnight.

Heat oven to 350 degrees. Roast Pork 2 hours, or until tender and juices run clear when meat is pierced with fork.

In small saucepan, combine schnapps, soy sauce, sugar and mustard. Simmer until slightly thickened.

Add peaches to pork roast 15 minutes before removing from oven.

Serve sliced pork with peaches and sauce.

Serves 8 - 10.

SAUCE FOR PEACHY PORK LOIN

In small bowl, combine 1 1/4 cups Peach Schnapps and 1 cup peach preserves.

Mix well.

BAKED HAM WITH PEACH GLAZE

1/3 CUP PEACH SCHNAPPS
3 1/2 - 4 Lb. Boneless Ham
Whole Cloves
1/3 Cup Each: Honey &
  Peach Preserves

1 Tbsp. Lemon Juice
1 Tbsp. Soy Sauce
Peach Slices
2 Tbsp. Dijon Mustard

Stud ham with cloves. Place on rack in shallow baking pan.

In small bowl, combine peach schnapps, honey, peach preserves, lemon juice and soy sauce.

Bake ham in oven, following directions on packaging. During the last 90 minutes of baking, brush ham with glaze.

Arrange peach slices on ham.

Top with glaze. Bake additional 10 minutes. Heat remaining glaze. Stir in drippings from baking pan and mustard.

Slice ham and serve with warm sauce.

Serves 6 to 8.

CORDIAL QUIZ QUESTION 1

What part of the Anise plant is used to make Anisette?

A) Seeds
B) Roots
C) Leaves
D) Bark

PEACH SCHNAPPS SCONES

1/4 CUP PEACH SCHNAPPS	3 Cups All-Purpose Flour
1 Cup Butter, Softened	1 Tbsp. Baking Powder
1/4 Cup Sugar	1/4 Tsp. Salt
3 Eggs	1/2 Almond Extract
	1/2 Cup Vanilla Yogurt

Prepare Peach Preserves in a smaller quantity by mixing 2 tablespoons of peach schnapps with 1/2 cup peach preserves. Set aside.

Cream butter and sugar until fluffly.

Add eggs, one at a time.

Mix flour, baking powder and salt until blended.

Add almond extract and yogurt.

Fold in peach mixture.

Drop 12 mounds of batter on ungreased baking sheet. Cover lightly. Refrigerate 45 minutes.

Bake in preheated 350 degree oven for 15 minutes.

Reduce heat to 325 degrees and bake 10 minutes. Remove from oven.

Sprinkle with remaining 1/4 cup peach schnapps.

Cool on rack and serve with Peach Schnapps Preserves. (See below.)

PEACH SCHNAPPS PRESERVES

In small bowl, combine **1 1/4 CUP PEACH SCHNAPPS** and 1 cup peach preserves.

Serve with Peach Schnapps Scones. (See above.)

FRUIT SALAD
WITH PEACH SCHNAPPS DRESSING

1/4 CUP PEACH SCHNAPPS   2 Tbsp. Sugar
1/2 Cup Mayonnaise   Dash Cinnamon
1/2 Cup Heavy Cream

In medium bowl, beat all ingredients until smooth.

Serve with assorted fresh fruit such as pineapple, oranges, grapes, bananas, pears and apples, or ready cut fresh fruit or refrigerated fresh fruit.

Garnish dressing with toasted coconut and chopped nuts, if desired.

Makes about 1 1/4 cups dressing.

BLACK RASPBERRY VINEGAR

A sprinkling adds zest to salads, especially chicken and fruit.
For each quart combine 2 cups red wine vinegar and **1 CUP BLACK RASPBERRY LIQUEUR**. Drop in **1 clove of garlic, peeled**. Cover tightly; let stand at least 2 hours before using. Note: Remove garlic clove as its flavor develops.

CORDIAL QUIZ QUESTION 2

Cordials sometime contain...
A) Gold Leaf
B) Pearls
C) Coral
D) All of the Above

CORNISH HENS
WITH BLACK RASPBERRY SAUCE

**3 TBSP. BLACK RASPBERRY
LIQUEUR
2 Cornish Hens, Split
2 Med. Cloves Garlic, cut in half
Salt and Freshly Ground Pepper
1/3 Cup Raspberry Jelly**

**1 Tbsp. Brown Sugar
1 Pkg. (6 oz.) Long Grain Rice
and Wild Rice with Seasonings
1/4 Cup Chopped Pecans
1/4 Cup fresh Raspberries**

Place hens on rack in shallow baking pan.

Rub inside and out with garlic.

Sprinkle with salt and pepper. Roast in 250 degree oven for 20 minutes.

In small saucepan, combine jelly, black raspberry liqueur and brown sugar. Simmer 5 minutes.

Brush hens with sauce.

Continue roasting 25 minutes or until tender.

Cook rice according to package directions.

Mix in nuts and berries.

Arrange hens on bed of rice.

Mix pan drippings from hens with remaining sauce.

Serve with hens and rice.

Serves 4.

RASPBERRY VINAIGRETTE SALAD DRESSING

1/2 CUP BLACK RASPBERRY
   LIQUEUR
1/4 Cup Balsamic Vinegar
1/4 Cup Chopped Onion
1 Med. Clove Garlic, Minced

1/2 Tsp. Salt
1 Tbsp. Lemon Juice
1 Tbsp. Dijon Mustard
3/4 Cup Olive Oil

In small saucepan, combine first 4 ingredients. Simmer 5 minutes. Blend in processor or blender until smooth.

Add remaining ingredients, except oil. Add oil in thin stream while continuing to blend until well mixed. Serve over greens of your choice.

Makes 1 1/3 cups.

ROAST DUCK WITH RASPBERRY SAUCE

1/2 CUP BLACK RASPBERRY
   LIQUEUR
4 -5 Lb. Duck
Salt and Ground Pepper
1 Small Orange, Quartered

1 Small Lemon, Quartered
1 Jar (12 Oz.) Seedless Raspberry
   Jam
2 Tbsp. fresh Lemon Juice
2 Tsp. Grated Lemon Zest

Heat oven to 400 degrees. With fork, pierce entire duck skin. Remove any excess fat. Sprinkle cavity with salt and pepper. Put fruit inside cavity and place duck on rack in shallow roasting pan. Pour 1/2 inch of water into pan. Roast 1 hour. Pour off all fat. Reduce heat to 325 degrees and roast for 1 1/2 to 2 hours or until brown and crisp.
Meanwhile, prepare sauce by heating jam over low heat until melted. Mix in black raspberry liqueur, lemon juice and zest. Simmer, uncovered, 10 minutes.
Serve with duck.
Serves 4.

ROAST CHICKEN
WITH RASPBERRY SAUCE

**This is a simple version of the Roast Duck Recipe
using chicken instead.**

Take a large oven-stuffer chicken, season with salt and pepper.

Brush lightly with oil and place in roasting pan filled with one inch of water.

Bake in 400 degree oven for about 1 1/2 hours or until chicken is crispy and brown with juices running clear and not red.

Make sure water does not evaporate. Add more if necessary.

After cooking, remove chicken from pan. Also remove any excess fat leaving drippings in pan.

Add to this 1 carrot, 1 onion, 1 tomato, coarsely chopped, and saute for 10 minutes.

Add 1 cup chicken broth.

Scrape pan to loosen all the brown bits and then strain this mixture into a container.

Melt 3 tablespoons sugar and 1 tablespoon butter in a saucepan and cook, stirring until the mixture is brown.

Add 1/3 cup cider vinegar and continue to cook until the mixture is reduced by half.

Pour in the sauce reserved in container and reduce heat to simmer.

Add one 10 ounce package of defrosted frozen raspberries and **1/4 CUP BLACK RASPBERRY LIQUEUR.**

Simmer for 10 minutes.

Serve over chicken.

CANDIED SWEET POTATOES

4 TBSP. RASPBERRY
   LIQUEUR
6 Sweet Potatoes
Salt and Paprika

3/4 Cup Brown Sugar
1 Tbsp. Grated Apple
2 Tbsp. Butter

Cook potatoes unpeeled in boiling water until tender.

Drain, peel and cut info half inch thick slices lengthwise.

Place in buttered, shallow baking dish.

Sprinkle with brown sugar, grated apple and Raspberry Liqueur.

Dot with butter, and bake uncovered in 375 degree oven for 20 minutes.

Serves 4.

BRANDIED CARROTS

3 TBSP. RASPBERRY
   LIQUEUR
1/4 Cup Brandy
24 Small Carrots

Juice of One Lemon
1/4 Cup Honey
2 Tbsp. Parsley, Finely Chopped
1 Tbsp. Butter

Put carrots in saucepan and cover with cold salted water. Bring to boil, reduce heat to simmer, cover and cook until tender.

Drain and arrange in buttered casserole.

Make syrup of liqueur, lemon juice, brandy and honey.

Pour over carrots and bake in 350 degree oven for 15 or 20 minutes.

Sprinkle with chopped parsley.

Serves 4.

PINEAPPLE BUTTERSCOTCH GLAZE AND SAUCE FOR HAM

1/4 CUP BUTTERSCOTCH
   SCHNAPPS
1 Jar (12 Oz.) Pineapple Jelly

1/4 Cup Horseradish
1 Tbsp. Dry Mustard
1 Can (8 Oz.) Crushed Pineapple

In a small saucepan, combine all ingredients except crushed pineapple.

Heat, stirring until mixture comes to a boil. Prepare ham of your choice following directions on ham. Baste ham with mixture every 10 minutes during last hour of baking. Mix in crushed pineapple with remaining glaze. Heat. Serve with sliced ham.

Makes glaze and sauce for 4 pound ham.

ZESTY CHEESE SPREAD

1/4 CUP BUTTERSCOTCH
   SCHNAPPS
1 Jar (12 Oz.) Apricot
   Preserves

1/2 Cup Horseradish
1/4 Cup Dijon Mustard
1/8 Tsp. Ground Red Pepper

Combine all ingredients. Cover and store in refrigerator up to 3 months. Mix and spoon over piece of cream cheese. Serve with crackers. Makes about 2 1/2 Cups.

BUTTERSCOTCH PRALINE SCONES

5 TBSP. BUTTERSCOTCH
  SCHNAPPS
1/4 Cup Sugar
3/4 Cup Pecans
2 1/4 Cups All-Purpose Flour
1/3 Cup Brown Sugar
2 Tsp. Baking Powder

1/2 Tsp. Salt
1/3 Butter, Chilled
2 Eggs
1/4 Cup Heavy Cream
1 Tsp. Pure Vanilla Extract
1 Egg Yolk

Lightly grease 9 inch circle on baking sheet.

In small saucepan, mix two tablespoons butterscotch schnapps and sugar.
Cook, stirring until sugar is dissolved.

Boil without stirring until mixture turns amber and thickens like caramel
(about 4 minutes).

Remove from heat. Stir in pecans. Spread mixture on baking sheet. Cool
15 minutes.

Chop praline into small pieces and set aside.

Preheat oven to 400 degrees. Lightly grease baking sheet.

In large bowl, mix flour, brown sugar, baking powder and salt. With knife
or pastry blender cut butter into flour mixture to resemble coarse crumbs.

In a small bowl, mix eggs, cream, vanilla and 2 tablespoons butterscotch
schnapps. Add liquid to flour mixture. Mix lightly. Add praline.

With floured hands turn dough onto floured surface. Pat into circle. Use
floured cutter, glass or knife and cut into 10 to 12 scones. Place on
prepared baking sheet.

Beat egg yolk with remaining butterscotch schnapps. Brush egg mixture
on top and sides of scones.

Bake 20 minutes or until toothpick comes out clean. Remove from
baking sheet onto wire rack.

Cool. Serve with Pecan Butterscotch Butter. Make 10 to 12 scones.

(For a complement to this recipe see PECAN BUTTERSCOTCH
BUTTER *on next page.)*

PECAN BUTTERSCOTCH BUTTER

Combine **2 TABLESPOONS BUTTERSCOTCH SCHNAPPS, 1/2 cup butter or margarine, softened**, and **3 tablespoons chopped pecans.**

Serve with recipe on previous page.

BUTTERY BARBECUE SAUCE

In medium saucepan, combine **3/4 CUPS BUTTERSCOTCH SCHNAPPS, 12 ounces chili sauce, 1/4 cup minced onion, 1 large clove garlic, minced, dash of Worcestershire sauce** and a **dash of ground red pepper.**

Simmer 5 minutes uncovered.

Use as a basting sauce.

YUMMY YOGURT SAUCE FOR FRUIT

3 TBSP. BUTTERSCOTCH SCHNAPPS	**Sliced bananas and green grapes**
8 Oz. Vanilla Yogurt	**Brown Sugar**

In small bowl, combine schnapps and yogurt.

Spoon over fruit. Sprinkle with sugar.

Makes about 1 1/4 Cups.

BUTTERSCOTCH BAKED BEANS

1/2 CUP BUTTERSCOTCH
  SCHNAPPS
2 Cans Baked Beans, Drained
1/3 Cup Each: Minced Onion
  and Ketchup

4 Slices Bacon, Partially Cooked
  and Cut Up
2 Tbsp. Brown Sugar
2 Tbsp. Dry Mustard

In large bowl combine all ingredients.

Pour into 1 and 1/2 quart casserole or bean pot. Bake uncovered in 275 degree oven for 45 minutes.

Serves about 4 people as a side dish.

CORDIAL QUIZ QUESTION 4

When should you drink an aperitif?

    A) Before a meal

    B) With a meal

    C) After a meal

    D) All night long

CAROL ANN'S CARROT DELIGHT

1/4 CUP ORANGE LIQUEUR
2 Tbsp. Butter or Margarine
1 Lb. Fresh or Frozen Whole
  Baby Carrots

1/2 Tsp. Salt
1 Tbsp. Brown Sugar
1 Tbsp. Freshly Grated Orange
  Rind

In medium skillet melt butter. Mix in remaining ingredients.

Cook covered over medium heat until carrots are tender.

Serves 4.

LIP SMACKING APPLE STUFFING

1/2 CUP ORANGE LIQUEUR
6 Tbsp. Butter or Margarine
1/2 Cup Each: Chopped Onion
  and Celery
6 Cups Seasoned Dry Bread
  Cubes

1 Egg, Beaten
1 Cup Sliced Almonds
1 Large Apple, Cored and
  Chopped
1 Tsp. Poultry Seasoning

In large skillet, melt butter.

Add onion and celery and cook until onion is softened.

Mix in remaining ingredients.

Add water or chicken broth if moister stuffing is desired.

Stuff 12 to 15 pound turkey or 2 large roasting chickens.

Follow poultry instructions on wrapper for roasting directions.

To bake stuffing as side dish, spoon into large greased baking dish.

Bake in 350 degree oven for 45 to 50 minutes.

CORDIAL QUIZ QUESTION 5

Green anise liqueur is also known as...

A) Nectar of the Gods

B) The Juice of Life

C) Oil of Fennel

D) Scandinavian Syrup

MINT MARINADE FOR LAMB

1/3 CUP PEPPERMINT
SCHNAPPS
2 Tbsp. Cooking Oil

1 Large Clove Garlic, Minced
6 Loin or Shoulder Lamb Chops
2 Tbsp. Dijon Mustard

Combine all ingredients except lamb. Place lamb in large plastic bag.

Pour liquid marinade over lamb. Secure plastic bag tightly.

Refrigerate several hours, turning occasionally.

Broil or grill, basting with marinade, until cooked as desired.

Serves 6.

CLUCK-CLUCK CHILI

3/4 CUP CAFE MOCHA
2 Tbsp. Cooking Oil
1 1/2 Lbs. Boneless Chicken
    Breasts, Cut in 1/2 inch pieces
1 Large Green Pepper, Chopped
2 Large Onions, Chopped
3 Large Cloves Garlic, Minced

12 Oz. Thick Hot Salsa
2 8 Oz. Whole Tomatoes, Chopped
6 Oz. Tomato Paste
3 Tbsp. Chili Powder
1 Tsp. Each: Salt and Oregano
15 Oz. Kidney Beans, Undrained
2 Stalks Celery, Sliced

Heat oil in large saucepan. Add chicken. Cook, stirring until chicken is lightly browned.

Add all ingredients except beans. Simmer, uncovered, 1 hour.

Mix in beans. Simmer 15 minutes.

Serve with sour cream, shredded cheese and sliced ripe olives.

Serves 8.

GREEN PEAS WITH MINT

1/4 CUP PEPPERMINT   10 Oz. Frozen Green Peas
SCHNAPPS   2 Tbsp. Butter or Margarine

In small saucepan, cook all ingredients, covered, 3 to 4 minutes or until peas are tender.

Serves 4.

SHERRY'S KAHLUA SOUFFLE

KAHLUA   4 Eggs
Lady Fingers   3 1/2 Tbsp. Sugar

Preheat oven 400 degrees. Line the top and side of souffle dish with lady fingers. Make sure that lady fingers are tightly together and place around dish vertically. Sprinkle liberally with Kahlua.

Separate the eggs and beat the yolks until they turn a light lemon color. Add sugar and keep beating then add 1 tablespoon of Kahlua. Beat egg white until stiff. Gently fold egg yolk into egg whites. Do not beat. Pour into souffle dish. Bake for ten minutes.

Serves 4.

CORDIAL QUIZ QUESTION 6

Which of these is not used to make Schnapps?

A) Molasses
B) Grain
C) Potatoes
D) Cactus

LUSCIOUS ORANGE VINAIGRETTE

1 1/2 TBSP. ORANGE LIQUEUR	2 Tbsp. Wine Vinegar
6 Juice Oranges	1 1/2 Tsp. Chopped Onion
7 Tbsp. Canola Oil	Salt and Pepper to taste
	2 Tbsp. Chopped Fresh Cilantro

Peel oranges and remove seeds. Slice horizontally and arrange on a platter.

In small bowl mix everything except cilantro. Pour over the oranges and sprinkle with the cilantro.

Serves 6.

SASSY SHRIMP L'ORANGE

4 TBSP. ORANGE LIQUEUR	2 Tbsp. Chopped Onion
1 Lb. Large Shrimp	1 Tbsp. Lemon Juice
4 Oranges	Salt and Pepper to taste
	Sugar

Combine liqueur and juice of 1orange in large bowl.

Clean and devein shrimp removing tail. Place in liqueur mixture and marinate for overnight.

Add lemon to chopped onion and set aside. Peal and remove pits from remaining oranges. Slice horizontally and add to shrimp. Also add marinated onion to shrimp.

Before serving place shrimp and marinade into wok. Add a very small amount of peanut oil. Stir fry the shrimp in the oil and marinade until shrimp turn pink. Do not overcook. While cooking add seasonings and sugar to taste.

Serve over brown rice.

Serves 6.

DOUBLE FRUIT SOUP

2 TBSP. ORANGE LIQUEUR	1 Orange
2 Cans Plain Tomato Soup Diluted with 2 cans water	4 Tbsp. Heavy Cream
	Grated Orange Zest

Place soup and water in medium saucepan. Stir thoroughly. Slowly simmer until hot.

Peel and remove pits from orange. Squeeze juice and add 2 tablespoons to soup.

Just before serving add liqueur. Pour into soup bowls and drop a dollop of whipped cream on top of each bowl. Sprinkle a little zest on top of cream.

Serves 4.

HIGH TIME HAM ROLLS

2 TBSP. ORANGE LIQUEUR	2 Oranges, peeled, seeded and diced
8 Oz. Small Curd Cottage Cheese	6 Slices Cooked Ham
	2 Tbsp. White Raisins

Soak raisins in liqueur until raisins plump up.

In small bowl mix cottage cheese with raisins and oranges. Place some of cheese mixture on each slice of ham.

Roll up ham and place on bed of fresh greens.

Drizzle a small amount of liqueur onto salad and garnish with orange slices.

Serves 3.

CORDIAL QUIZ QUESTION 7

Which spirit is never used as a
base for liqueurs?

A) Wine

B) Rum

C) Cognac

D) Whiskey

ESCALOPE ESCAPADE

4 TBSP. ORANGE
   LIQUEUR
4 Veal Escalopes
1/4 Cup Flour
2 Tbsp. Olive Oil

2 Oranges
1/3 Cup Chicken Stock
Salt and Pepper to Taste
Parsley to Garnish

Dip veal lightly in flour. Add oil to skillet. Place veal in heated oil and
brown lightly on both sides. Remove and set aside.

In same saucepan add the juice of 1 orange, 1 teaspoon of the zest,
liqueur and chicken stock. Reheat and simmer until slightly thickened.

If sauce is too thin, add a little flour and stir.

Return veal to skillet and add salt and pepper. Cover and simmer for
about 15 minutes.

Carefully place veal onto serving platter. Pour sauce over meat and
garnish with fresh parsley leaves and grated orange zest.

Serves 4.

ROYAL FLAMBEED
STRAWBERRIES

6 TBSP. ORANGE LIQUEUR   **18 Lg. Whole Strawberries**
6 Tbsp. Brandy   **1 1/2 Cups Heavy Cream,**
1 Cup Sugar   **Whipped**

Wash and remove green tops from strawberries. Pat dry.

In small saucepan heat liqueur, brandy and sugar. Warm just until sugar is slightly dissolved. Do not overheat.

Place strawberries in fire-proof dish. Pour liqueur mixture over strawberries and set aflame. Gently shake the dish until the flame goes out.

Serve immediately with whipped cream.

Serves 6.

ANSWERS TO CORDIAL QUIZ

1) A - Seeds

2) D - All of the Above

3) C - Sugar Content

4) A - Before a Meal

5) C - Oil of Fennel

6) D - Cactus

7) A - Wine

LIQUEUR
Laced
Desserts

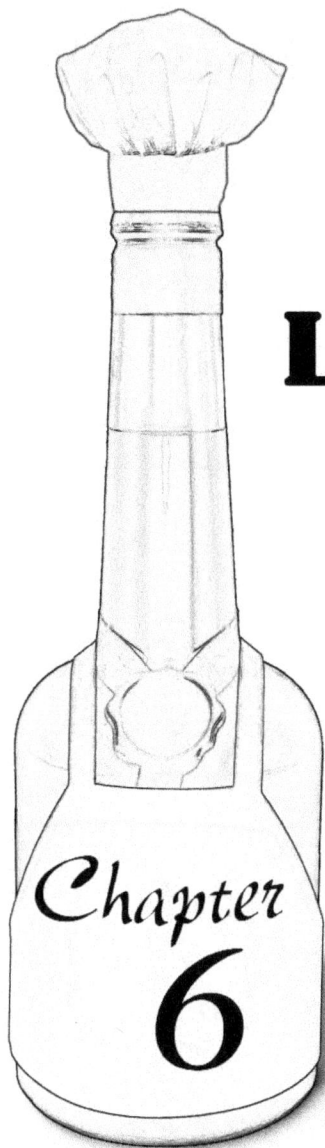

Chapter 6

The effect of using LIQUEURS in desserts can range from sumptuous to lavish to outright decadent.

Because of their inherent sweetness and flavorings LIQUEURS are a natural ingredient in dessert recipes.

145

MAX'S MACADAMIA NUT PIE

CRUST

1 1/2 Cups Shortbread
Cookie Crumbs

1/2 Cup Chopped Macadamia Nuts
1/4 Cup Melted Butter

Mix all ingredients thoroughly. Press on bottom and sides of 9 inch pie pan.

Chill while preparing filling.

FILLING

3/4 CUP WHITE CHOCOLATE
LIQUEUR
2 Cups Heavy Cream
1/4 Cup Confectioners Sugar

1 Tsp. Pure Vanilla Extract
1/2 Cup Each: Macadamia Nuts,
Toasted Coconut, and
Shortbread Cookie Crumbs

Whip white chocolate liqueur, heavy cream, sugar and vanilla until stiff. Fold in remaining ingredients. Pour into crust.

Place in freezer several hours or overnight.

Garnish with shaved white chocolate and macadamia nuts.

Serves 8.

HARLEQUIN PARFAITS

2 TBSP. AMARETTO
1 Pint Coffee Ice Cream

1 Pint Chocolate Ice Cream
Toasted Slivered Almonds

In 4 to 6 parfait glasses, alternate spoonfuls of coffee ice cream and chocolate ice cream. Pour Arnaretto in each parfait glass. Sprinkle with toasted slivered almonds.

Serves 4 to 6.

CHOCOLATE LOVER'S CHEESECAKE

CRUST

1 3/4 Cups Graham Cracker
    Crumbs

2 Tbsp. Sugar
1/3 Cup Melted Butter

Combine all ingredients. Press evenly on bottom and sides of 9" spring form pan.

Set aside while preparing filling.

FILLING

1/2 CUP DARK CHOCOLATE
    LIQUEUR
6 Oz. Semi Sweet Chocolate
1 1/2 Lbs Cream Cheese,
    Softened

1 Cup Sugar
2 Tsp. Pure Vanilla Extract
4 Eggs
1/2 Cup Heavy Cream
1/4 Cup Melted Butter

Melt chocolate over hot (not boiling) water. Remove from heat. Slowly mix in liqueur, beating continuously with wire whisk. Blend until smooth. Set aside.

With mixer, beat cream cheese, sugar and vanilla until smooth. Beat in eggs, one at a time. Mix in cream and butter just until blended.

Pour half of cheese mixture in crust. Spoon half of liqueur mixture onto cheese mixture. Spread with remaining cheese mixture. Spoon remaining liqueur mixture on top.

With knife cut through filling to create marble effect.

Place pan on cookie sheet. Bake in preheated 350 degree oven for 55 minutes. Turn off oven. Let cheesecake remain in oven for 1 hour. Remove from oven.

Cool on wire rack at room temperature. Chill.

Serves 12.

LIQUEUR QUIZ QUESTION 1

Sloe Gin can be correctly classified as....

A) Brandy

B) Gin

C) Liqueur

D) None of the Above

SWEETHEART BROWNIES

1/2 CUP CHOCOLATE LIQUEUR	1/2 Tsp. Salt
5 Oz. Unsweetened Chocolate	2 1/2 Cups Chopped Walnuts
1/2 Cup Butter	2 Cups of Sugar
1 Tbsp. Instant Coffee	1 Tsp. Vanilla Extract
5 Eggs	1/2 Cup Sifted All-Purpose Flour

In double boiler, melt chocolate and butter.

When smooth, add instant coffee and set aside to cool.

Beat eggs and salt together until slightly fluffy. Add sugar gradually and beat until mixture is ribbony (about 10 minutes).

Add vanilla extract, liqueur and cooled chocolate to eggs while beating on low speed.

Fold in sifted flour until just incorporated, then fold in nuts. Pour batter onto greased, floured and parchment lined 11" by 17" baking pan.

Place in preheated 450 degree oven, lowering temperature to 400 degrees.

Bake 20 to 22 minutes or until toothpick inserted in center remains clean.

Makes 20 2" by 3" brownies.

SUNDAY SOUFFLE GLACE

1/2 CUP CHOCOLATE LIQUEUR	1 Tbsp. Instant Coffee
	2 Tbsp. Cocoa Powder
8 Eggs	1 Tsp. Vanilla Extract
1 Cup Sugar	3 1/2 Cups Heavy Cream

Fold waxed paper or parchment paper lengthwise, spray with vegetable coating and secure around 1 quart souffle dish to make three inch standing collar.

In stainless bowl over simmering water, whip eggs, sugar, coffee and cocoa powder until mixture is thickened and hangs in hoop of wire whip.

Remove from heat, add vanilla and liqueur. Cool.

Whip cream and fold in gently in four batches. Pour mixture into greased and collared souffle dish. Freeze.

To serve, remove collar and garnish with shaved chocolate.

Serves 12.

LIQUEUR QUIZ QUESTION 2

The word "Liqueur" comes from the Latin "Liquifacere" which means....
A) To stimulate
B) To sweeten
C) To dissolve
D) To intoxicate

DECADENT STRAWBERRY TORTE

1 1/2 CUPS CHOCOLATE
   LIQUEUR
2 Envelopes Unflavored
   Gelatin
1/2 Cup Cold Water
3 Eggs Yolks
1/2 Cup of Sugar
1/4 Tsp. Salt

1/2 Cup of Milk, Scalded
1 Tsp. Vanilla Extract
10 Oz. frozen Strawberries,
   Pureed (Unsweetened)
1 Cup Heavy Cream
1 9" Sponge cake
1 Qt. Fresh Strawberries, Hulled
Whipped Cream

Soften gelatin in water, set aside.

In double boiler, cook egg yolks, sugar, salt and milk until slightly thickened.

Remove from heat, add gelatin mixture and stir until dissolved.

Add vanilla, liqueur and strawberry puree, chill until slightly thickened and mixture mounds in a spoon.

Whip cream until stiff and fold into strawberry mixture.

To assemble, place cake in 9" greased spring form pan, sprinkle with liqueur, cover with strawberries, hulled side down and top with strawberry mixture.

Refrigerate several hours before serving.

Garnish with whipped cream and fresh strawberries.

Serves 12.

151

ANGEL CHOCOLATE PIE

1/2 CUP CHOCOLATE LIQUEUR	1/4 Soft Butter or Margarine
2 TBSP. CHOCOLATE LIQUEUR	1 Tbsp. Sugar
1 1/2 Cups Chocolate Cookie Crumbs	1 Qt. Chocolate Ice Cream
	1 Cup Heavy Cream
	Chocolate Sprinkles

In a bowl, mix crumbs, butter or margarine and sugar. Press mixture firmly into an ungreased 9" pie pan. Chill.

Soften ice cream. Stir in liqueur. Pour mixture into chilled pie shell and freeze until hard.

In a bowl, mix heavy cream and liqueur and beat until stiff. Pile whipped cream in mounds around outer edge of pie. Decorate with chocolate sprinkles. Freeze until ready to serve.

Makes 1 9" pie.

SUNDAY NIGHT SUNDAES

1/4 CUP ORANGE LIQUEUR	2 Tbsp. Orange Marmalade
11 Oz. Canned Mandarin Oranges	1 Pint Vanilla Ice Cream
2 Tbsp. Syrup from Oranges	Toasted Sliced Almonds

Drain mandarin oranges, reserving 2 tablespoons syrup.

In a small saucepan, combine reserved syrup, orange marmalade and Amaretto. Add mandarin oranges and simmer for 5 to 7 minutes.

Serve over vanilla ice cream. Top with toasted sliced almonds. Serve immediately.

Serves 4.

ALMOND LIQUEUR COOKIES

1/4 CUP ALMOND LIQUEUR   2/3 Cup All-Purpose Flour
2/3 Cup Butter   1/2 Cup Finely Chopped Almonds
2 Cups Uncooked Quick Oats   1/4 Cup Corn Syrup
1 Cup Sugar   1/2 Tsp. Salt

Preheat oven to 275 degrees.

Foil-line cookie sheets.

In medium saucepan, melt butter. Remove from heat.

Stir in quick oats, sugar, flour, almonds, corn syrup, 1/4 cup almond liqueur and salt.

Drop rounded teaspoons 2 inches apart onto prepared cookie sheets; spread each to make thin. Bake 8 to 11 minutes, until golden.

Cool completely on cookie sheets.

Peel off foil. Spread filling on flat side of 1/2 the cookies.

Top with remaining cookies.

Makes 2 1/2 Dozen.

FILLING

1/4 CUP ALMOND LIQUEUR   1/2 Cup Butter
1 1/2 Cups Chocolate Chips

In medium heavy gauge saucepan over low heat, melt butter with 1/4 cup almond liqueur.

Remove from heat.

Stir in 1 1/2 cups chocolate chips.

Cool to room temperature.

LET'S GO NUTS PIE

CRUST: In small heavy saucepan, melt 1/2 cup semisweet chocolate chips and 3 tablespoons butter over low heat.

Stir in 18 crushed chocolate chip cookies. Press mixture into 9" pie pan. Refrigerate.

SAUCE: In medium heavy saucepan melt 1 1/2 cups semisweet chocolate chips with 1/2 cup heavy cream and 2 tablespoons butter.

When melted, stir in **2 TABLESPOONS ALMOND LIQUEUR.**

FILLING: In large mixing bowl, beat 1 quart vanilla ice cream and **2 TABLESPOONS ALMOND LIQUEUR..** Spread 1/2 cup sauce on bottom of crust. Spoon filling over sauce. freeze. Refrigerate remaining sauce. Let pie stand at room temperature 5 to 10 minutes before serving.

Serve with remaining sauce and whipped cream.

Serves 8.

NUTS TO YOU
CHEESE BARS

CRUST: Preheat oven to 350 degrees. In large saucepan melt 1 1/4 cups butter.

Remove from heat and stir in 3 1/2 cups graham cracker crumbs, 1 cup slivered almonds, 1/2 cup sugar and **1/4 CUP ALMOND LIQUEUR.**

Press mixture info 15 1/2" x 10 1/2" x 1 " baking pan. Bake 10 to 12 minutes. Set aside.

FILLING: In large mixing bowl, beat two 8 ounce packages cream cheese and 1/2 cup sugar until well blended. Add 2 eggs, one at a time. Stir in **1/2 CUP ALMOND LIQUEUR.** Pour over crust.

Bake additional 20 to 25 minutes until set. Cool completely on wire rack.

Refrigerate before serving. Cut into bars.

Makes 6 dozen.

BUTTERY BRUNCH CAKE

4 TBSP. ALMOND LIQUEUR, Divided
1 Cup Butter or Margarine, Divided
2 Tbsp. Water
2 Cups All-Purpose Flour

2 Eggs
1 1/2 Cups Confectioners Sugar
2 Tbsp. Butter or Margarine, Softened
1 Cup Water

Heat oven to 350 degrees.

With knife or pastry blender, cut 1/3 cup butter into 1 cup flour. Sprinkle with water. With fork, stir and form into ball. Divide ball in half. Pat into 2 strips, about 12 x 2 inches each on ungreased baking sheet. Set aside.

In medium saucepan, heat 1/2 cup butter and 1 cup water to rolling boil. Remove from heat and stir in 2 tablespoons almond liqueur and 1 cup flour. Stir vigorously over low heat.

Beat in eggs, one at a time, until smooth and glossy. Divide in half. Spread each half over prepared strips.

Bake 55 minutes or until topping is crisp and brown. Cool.

Combine remaining 2 tablespoons almond liqueur, sugar and butter. Frost. Sprinkle with chopped almonds, if desired.

Serves 8 to 9.

LIQUEUR QUIZ QUESTION 3

Liqueurs are not "aged" but rather undergo...

A) "Resting stages"
B) "Maturity periods"
C) "Hyperbolic intervals"
D) "40 winks"

TIPSY TERRI'S TRIFLE

1/2 CUP ALMOND LIQUEUR
3/4 Cup Sugar
3 Tbsp. Cornstarch
2 Cups Heavy Cream, Divided
1 Cup Milk
5 Egg Yolks
1 10 to 12 Oz. Pound Cake

1/4 Cup ALMOND LIQUEUR
2 Cups Seasonal Fresh Fruits
    (Raspberries, Strawberries, etc.)
1 16 Oz. Can Sliced Peaches,
    Well Drained
Fresh Fruit to Garnish
Sliced Almonds to Garnish

In large heavy saucepan, stir sugar and cornstarch. Gradually stir in 1 cup heavy cream, milk and 1/2 cup almond liqueur.

Stirring constantly, cook over medium heat until mixture begins to boil. Reduce heat to low.

In small mixing bowl, beat egg yolks until lemon colored. Stir in 3/4 cup milk mixture. Quickly stir egg mixture into saucepan.

Stirring constantly, cook over low heat until mixture thickens.

Transfer to large bowl and cover surface with plastic wrap. Refrigerate.

In large mixing bowl, beat remaining 1 cup heavy cream until stiff peaks form. Fold into custard mixture.

Cut pound cake into 1/4 inch thick slices. Cut each slice in thirds lengthwise.

Brush one side of pound cake with remaining almond liqueur.

In glass bowl, add 1/3 of custard mixture. Layer 1/2 the pound cake and 1/2 peaches.

Repeat with remaining ingredients.

Garnish with sliced almonds.

Serves 8.

APRICOT CHEESE PIE

1/4 CUP ALMOND LIQUEUR	3 Eggs
1 Tbsp. Margarine	Pinch of Salt
1/2 Cup Graham Cracker Crumbs	1/2 Cup Each: Golden Raisins and Finely Chopped Apricots
1 Lb. Pot Style Cottage Cheese	Ground Cinnamon
	1/2 Cup Sugar

Spread margarine over bottom of a non-stick 8" pie pan. Sprinkle on graham cracker crumbs; press firm over bottom of pan.

Combine cheese, liqueur, eggs, sugar and salt in blender or food processor container. Process until smooth scraping down sides of container with rubber scraper.

Pour half of this filling mixture into pie pan. Sprinkle raisins and apricots evenly over filling. Pour on remaining filling, covering all fruit. Sprinkle with cinnamon.

Bake in preheated 325 degree oven for 45 to 55 minutes, or until filling is set. Cool before serving.

Serves 8.

BUTTERSCOTCH BANANA PIE

CRUST: Combine 1/3 cup melted butter or margarine, **2 TBSP. BUTTERSCOTCH SCHNAPPS**, 2 tbsp. brown sugar and 2 1/4 cups crushed shortbread cookies. Reserve 1/2 cup crumbs and set aside. Press remaining crumbs on bottom and sides of 8 inch pie plate.

FILLING: Beat 3/4 cup heavy cream, 3/4 cup milk, **1/4 CUP BUTTERSCOTCH SCHNAPPS** and 1 package instant vanilla pudding and pie filling for 2 minutes. Peel and slice 1 banana. Layer banana slices on bottom of cruet. Pour in filling. Sprinkle with reserved crumbs. Chill. Garnish with whipped cream.

Serves 6 to 8.

POACHED FRESH FRUIT

3/4 CUP PEACH SCHNAPPS
1 Jar (10 Oz.) Currant Jelly
1 Stick Cinnamon
5 Whole Cloves

1 Strip Lemon Peel (2 Inches)
4 Plums, Cut in Half
2 Pears, Cored and Cut in Half
2 Peaches, Peeled and Cut in Half

In large skillet, melt jelly.

Mix in peach schnapps, cinnamon, cloves and lemon. Stir in fruit.

Poach about 15 minutes or until fruit is tender. Cool.

Serves 4.

GOLDEN APPLE TART

1/2 CUP BUTTERSCOTCH
   SCHNAPPS
9" Pastry Shell
4 Large Tart Apples, Peeled
   and Thickly Sliced
2 Tbsp. Butter

2 Eggs, Beaten
3/4 Cup Heavy Cream
1/4 Brown Sugar
1 Tsp. Vanilla Extract
1/8 Tsp. Nutmeg

Heat oven to 400 degrees.

Partially bake pastry shell 5 minutes. Remove from oven and set aside.

In skillet, cook apples in butter, just until tender. Arrange in even layer in shell.

Combine remaining ingredients. Pour over apples.

Bake in 350 degree oven for 45 minutes or until custard is set and pie is golden brown.

Serve with whipped cream.

Serves 6 to 8.

PEACH ALMOND CRUNCH CAKE

3/4 CUP PEACH SCHNAPPS   1/3 Cup Cooking Oil
1 Pkg. 2 Layer Yellow Cake Mix   1/2 Cup water
3 Eggs   3/4 Cup Slivered Almonds

Heat oven to 325 degrees.

Grease and flour 12 cup bundt pan. Sprinkle nuts on pan. Mix all remaining cake ingredients and beat 2 minutes in electric mixer. Pour over nuts in prepared pan.

Bake for 1 hour. Cool in pan on rack for 10 minutes. Invert on serving plate.

GLAZE: In medium saucepan, place 3/4 cup peach schnapps, 1/2 cup butter or margarine and 1/2 cup sugar. Bring mixture to a boil for 15 minutes.

Prick top of cake with fork and drizzle glaze over cake. Cool.

Serves 10 to 12.

LIQUEUR QUIZ QUESTION 4

In the Middle Ages it was required for liqueurs to be served at all...

A) Coronations
B) Knightings
C) Treaty Signings
D) Executions

PEPPERMINT PIE

CRUST

Heat oven to 250 degrees.

Combine 2 cups chocolate cookie crumbs, 1/2 cup butter or margarine and **1 TBSP. PEPPERMINT SCHNAPPS**. Set aside 1/2 cup of mixture. Press remaining mixture on bottom and sides of 9" pie plate.

Bake for 5 minutes.

FILLING

In medium saucepan, over low heat, melt 24 large marshmellows in 1/2 cup milk. Remove from heat.

Stir in **1/4 CUP PEPPERMINT SCHNAPPS** and 4 drops red food coloring. Chill until thickened.

Fold 1 cup heavy cream, whipped, into marshmellow mixture. Pour into prepared crust.

Sprinkle with reserved crumbs.

Chill several hours.

Serve with whipped cream and garnish with mint leaves if available.

MILK CHOCOLATE DESSERT SAUCE

2/3 CUP PEPPERMINT SCHNAPPS
4 Oz. semi-sweet chocolate, Chopped

2/3 Cup Sugar
1/4 Cup Butter or Margarine
1 Tsp. Pure Vanilla Extract

In medium saucepan, combine all ingredients, except vanilla.

Heat, stirring until butter is melted. Cook for 4 to 5 minutes until slightly thickened. Remove from heat.

Stir in vanilla.

Serve over ice cream or as dessert fondue sauce with fruit.

STRAWBERRY PARFAIT GRANDE

In a large saucepan mix 1 tablespoon unflavored gelatin, 1 tablespoon flour and 3/4 cup sugar.

Beat 3 cups heavy cream and 5 egg yolks together and stir into the gelatin mixture.

Stirring constantly with a wire whisk, cook mixture over medium heat for 10 minutes.

Remove from heat, add 1 tablespoon vanilla.

Pour into large bowl and stir in grated peel of one orange and **1/4 CUP STRAWBERRY LIQUEUR**. Chill to thicken.

Puree in blender one pint fresh strawberries. Whip 1 cup heavy cream and fold into strawberries. Fold this into lightly thickened chilled cream mixture.

Spoon into champagne glasses. Chill until firm.

Garnish with fresh strawberries.

Serves 6.

MAGNIFICENT MELBA SAUCE

In a saucepan, combine one 10 ounce package of frozen raspberries, 1/2 cup currant jelly, 1/4 cup sugar.

Stir over moderate heat until boiling.

Add 1 tsp. cornstarch. Then simmer gently for 10 minutes.

Add **1/2 CUP STRAWBERRY LIQUEUR** and 1/2 teaspoon lemon juice.

Strain and chill before serving.

Excellent sauce over fresh fruit or ice cream.

MYSTIC MOUSSE

4 OZ. RASPBERRY LIQUEUR   **1 Cup Heavy Cream**
6 Egg Yolks   **9 Tbsp. Sugar**

Beat the egg yolks, sugar and Raspberry Liqueur together until they are thick and pale yellow.

In another bowl, beat the cream until stiff. Fold the cream into the egg yolks until mixture is completely blended.

Pour into dessert cups and place in freezer for one hour. Serve directly from freezer.

Serves 2.

LIQUEUR QUIZ QUESTION 5
What is the name of the process in which flavor is imparted to liqueurs?
A) Infusion
B) Diffusion
C) Transfusion
D) Confusion

RASPBERRY BERRY BOWL

In serving bowl, place 8 cups fresh strawberries, raspberries and blueberries.

Pour **1/2 CUP** chilled **BLACK RASPBERRY LIQUEUR** over fruit.

Chill.

Serves 10.

BLACK RASPBERRY DESSERT SAUCE

In medium saucepan, combine **1/2 CUP BLACK RASPBERRY LIQUEUR**, 2 packages (12 oz. each) frozen raspberries, thawed, pureed and strained and 1 tablespoon cornstarch.

Stir until cornstarch is dissolved.

Cook, stirring, until mixture comes to a boil.

Chill.

Serve as sauce for sliced oranges, strawberries, peach melba or pound cake.

Makes 2 1/2 cups.

FLAMBEED CHERRIES

2 OZ. RASPBERRY LIQUEUR   **1/2 Cup Sugar**
1 Can Cherries, Pitted and   **Juice of 1 Lemon**
  Drained   **Juice of 1 Orange**
1 Cup of the Cherry Juice   **1 Oz. Butter**
1 Oz. Brandy

Place the butter and sugar in a saucepan and heat until golden.

Add the lemon, orange and cherry juices and cook until smooth.

Add the cherries and liqueur and simmer for a few more minutes.

Then add the Brandy and ignite.

Be sure not to bum yourself!

Serve over crepes or vanilla ice cream.

Serves 8.

LIQUEUR QUIZ QUESTION 6

When used medicinally, a liqueur is referred to as a...

A) Balm

B) Tincture

C) Elixer

D) Potion

BAKED APPLES DELUXE

1 CUP CRANBERRY LIQUEUR
6 Large Baking Apples
1/4 Cup Each: Raisins and
    Chopped Pecans

2 Whole Cloves
1/2 Stick Cinnamon
1/4 Tsp. Mace
1/2 Cup Sugar

Core apples and peel 1 inch skin around top of apples. Place in 2 quart casserole. Set aside.

Mix sugar, raisins and pecans. Fill center of apples with mixture.

Mix cloves, liqueur, cinnamon and mace. Pour over apples and place in 375 degree oven. Bake for 45 minutes or until apples are tender.

While apples are cooking, in small bowl mix 3 ounces cream cheese, softened, 3 tablespoons heavy cream and 1 tablespoon sugar.

Serve topping over warm baked apples.

Serves 6.

CRANBERRY DESSERT SAUCE

In small saucepan, combine **1/2 CUP CRANBERRY LIQUEUR,** 1/2 cup brown sugar and 1 can (8 oz.) whole cranberry sauce.

Bring to boil. Cool.

Mix in nuts. Serve over sliced cake, ice cream or sherbet.

Makes 1 3/4 cups.

CRANBERRY NUT LOAF

1/4 CUP CRANBERRY LIQUEUR	**1/4 Cup Butter or Margarine, Softened**
1 Cup Flour	**1 Can (8 oz.) Whole Cranberry Sauce**
3/4 Tsp. Baking Powder	
1/2 Tsp. Salt	**1/2 Tsp. Finely Grated Orange Rind**
1/4 Tsp. Baking Soda	
1 Egg	**1/4 Cup Coarsely Chopped Pecans**

Sift flour, baking powder, salt and soda.

In food processor, cream butter, sugar and egg. Add cranberry sauce, orange rind and 2 tablespoons liqueur.

Mix in dry ingredients just until blended. Quickly mix in nuts. Pour into 2 greased 5 11/16" x 2 1/4" x 2" foil loaf pans.

Bake in preheated oven. Pour remaining liqueur over top of loaves.

Cool 10 minutes. Remove from pans. Place on rack.

Cool completely.

Wrap tightly.

Store 24 hours.

CRANBERRY COFFEE CAKE

1/4 CUP CRANBERRY
  LIQUEUR
1/4 Cup Butter or Margarine,
  Melted
2 Tbsp. Brown Sugar
1/4 Cup Slivered Almonds

1/4 Tsp. Cinnamon
1 Can (8 Oz.) Whole Cranberry
  Sauce
1 Can (8 Oz.) Refrigerated
  Buttermilk Biscuits

In 9" round baking pan, mix butter, liqueur, brown sugar, almonds, cinnamon and cranberry sauce. Arrange biscuits on top.

Bake in preheated 400 degree oven for 10 to 15 minutes or until brown. Invert on plate immediately and serve warm.

Serves 6 to 8.

IRISH CREAM PIE

1/4 CUP CREAM STYLE
  LIQUEUR
1 Envelope plain Gelatin
1 Cup Boiling Water
1 Cup Part-Skim Ricotta
  Cheese

4 Serving Envelope Vanilla or
  Chocolate Pudding Mix
Pinch of Salt
Ready to Fill Graham Cracker or
  Chocolate Cookie Pie shell
1/2 Cup Cold Skim Milk

Sprinkle gelatin on liqueur in blender or food processor container.

Wait 1 minute until gelatin is soft then add boiling water. Cover and process until gelatin is dissolved.

Scrape sides of container with rubber scraper. Add ricotta and milk; process smooth.

Add pudding mix and salt and process until smooth. Spoon into pie shell and chill until firm.

Serve with Whipped Cream.

Serves 8.

GRANDMOTHER'S SECRET INGREDIENT APPLE PIE

1/4 CUP ORANGE LIQUEUR	1 Tsp. Pumpkin Pie Spice or
Single Pie Crust	1/2 Tsp. Ground Cinnamon
6 Cups Thinly Sliced Apples	Pinch of Each: Nutmeg, Clove,
3 Tbsp. Golden Raisins	Allspice, ginger
1 Tbsp. Cornstarch	1 Cup Sugar

Roll out pastry as thin as possible and use ft to line a non-stick 8 or 9 inch pie plate sprayed with cooking spray.

Stir remaining ingredients in large bowl. Pour into crust. Cover apple filling with an inverted slightly smaller pie pan or a circle of aluminum foil cut to fit.

Bake in preheated 400 degree oven until crust is golden and apple slices are tender.

Remove from oven and serve warm or chilled.

Serves 8.

LIQUEUR QUIZ QUESTION 7
What is a "Wassail"?
A) A Toast

B) A Liqueur

C) A Party

D) All of the Above

HAPPY HAMILTON'S
SOUR CREAM CAKE

1/2 CUP ALMOND LIQUEUR	1 Pkg. Butter-Recipe Cake Mix
2 Eggs, Separated	1 Cup Sour Cream
1/2 Cup Brown Sugar	1/2 Cup Water
3/4 Cup Coconut	2 Eggs
1/2 Cup Ground Nuts	

Preheat oven to 350 degrees.

Grease 10 inch tube pan with shortening.

In a small bowl beat 2 egss whites until foamy. Add brown sugar and beat for about 3 minutes.

Fold in coconut and ground nuts. Spread on the bottom and sides of the greased pan up to about 1 inch from the top.

In a large bowl blend together the cake mix, sour cream, liqueur, water, egss and the 2 egg yolks. Beat vigorously for two minutes. Pour into the prepared pan.

Bake at 350 degrees for one hour or until an inserted toothpick comes out clean. Let cool.

GLAZE

2 TBSP. ALMOND LIQUEUR	1 Tbsp. Corn Syrup
1 Cup Sifted Powdered Sugar	3 Teaspoons Water
2 Tbsp. Cocoa	2 Teaspoons Ground Nuts
1 Tbsp. Butter or Margarine	6 Halved Maraschino Cherries

In small pan blend all ingredients except nuts, cherries and liqueur. Bring to a boil. Remove from heat and add liqueur.
Spoon over top of cake and allow some to run down sides.
Sprinkle with nuts and garnish with cherries.

About 16 servings.

OH MY GOSH GANACHE

A MELT IN YOUR MOUTH TOPPING
FOR CAKES OR MAKING CANDY TRUFFLES

2 TBS. PEPPERMINT SCHNAPPS   **16 oz. semisweet chocolate,**
1 ½ cups heavy cream   **chopped finely**

Place chopped chocolate in large bowl.

In small saucepan, add heavy cream. Bring to a boil, stirring constantly. Immediately pour hot cream over chocolate. Mix until all chocolate is completely melted. Add liqueur and stir well.

Ganache will appear thin after mixing and can be used in several ways. Cool for about 12 minutes and spoon over cake for a thin glaze. If you prefer frosting your cake, let ganache stand at room temperate for approximately 4 hours.

For truffles, place the garnache in refrigerator until firm. Scoop into balls and roll them in nuts, coconut or sweet powdered chocolate.

STIR CRAZY FRUITCAKE

1 TBSP. ORANGE LIQUEUR   **5 Tbsp. Brown Sugar**
1 Cup Self-Rising Flour   **1 Tsp. Pumpkin Pie Spice**
1 Egg   **1/2 Cup Fruit Bits (or Diced**
1/2 Cup Milk   **Dried Fruits)**

Sprinkle unsifted flour into an 8" round or square cake pan. Add the egg, milk, sugar and spice.
Stir together with a mixing spoon or rubber spatula until mixed. Stir in fruit and liqueur. Level the surface with a rubber spatula, and bake uncovered in a preheated 350 degree oven for 20 to 25 minutes until done (when a knife inserted in the center comes out clean).

Serve warm or cold.

ANSWERS TO LIQUEUR QUIZ

1) C - Liqueur

2) C - To Dissolve

3) A - Resting Stages

4) C - Treaty Signings

5) A - Infusion

6) B - Tincture

7) D - All of the Above

PUNCHES
With a Kick

Chapter 7

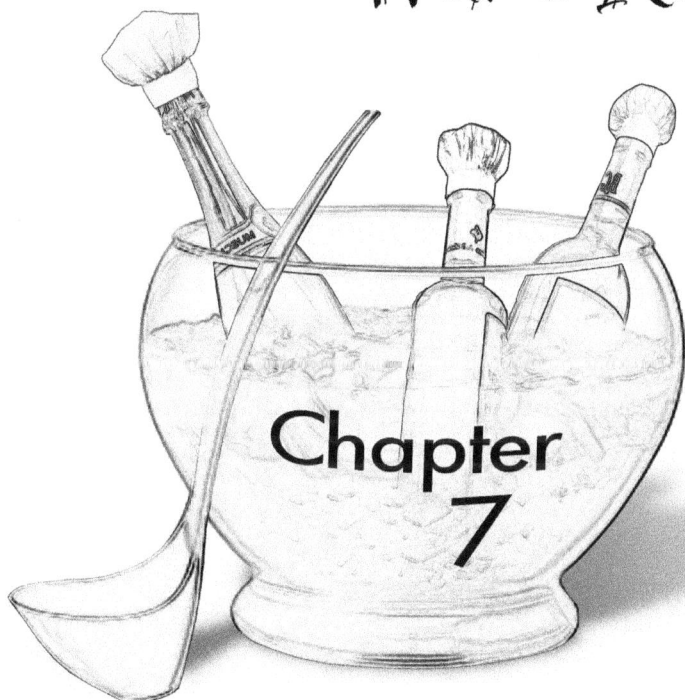

In any PUNCH recipe, the alcohol quantity is listed merely as a suggestion. When determining the strength of the mixture, the punch-maker should consider the personal preferences of the imbibers as well as the nature of the occasion.

A conservative mixologist can safely reduce the recommended quantities of alcohol without severe detriment to the PUNCH'S flavor.
A daring preparer might want to use for guidance this quote credited to Mark Twain: " While too much of most anything is never good, too much alcohol is just right."

GIN SWIZZLE

1 PINT GIN OR VODKA   4 Oz. Lime Juice
2 Oz. Sugar Syrup   10 Dashes Bitters

Stir until foamy.

Add ice and pour into cocktail glasses.

Serves 10.

MIDNIGHT PUNCH

1 QT. GIN   1/2 Pint Grapefruit Juice
1/2 Pint Tea

Mix ingredients in punch bowl with a large block of ice.

Just prior to serving, pour in 4 bottles of pre-chilled ginger ale.

Serves 15.

PINEAPPLE PUNCH

8 OZ. VODKA   Juice of 9 Lemons
1 1/2 QTS. DRY WHITE WINE   5 Dashes Bitters
1 Oz. Pineapple Syrup   1 Oz. Grenadine
1 Oz. Maraschino   1 Qt. Soda

Combine in punch bowl with 1 quart chilled soda.

Set bowl in bed of crushed ice.

Decorate with pineapple.

Serves 10.

ISLAND PUNCH

2 QTS. LIGHT RUM	1 1/2 Pints Lemon Juice
1 QT. COGNAC	3/4 Lb. Sugar
4 OZ. PEACH BRANDY	2 1/2 Pints Water

Dissolve sugar in part of the water in punch bowl. Add the lemon juice and balance of water. Stir thoroughly.

Add the liquor. Allow mixture to stand for 2 to 3 hours, stirring from time to time. Place large block of ice in the bowl, stir to cool, and serve in punch cups.

Serves 20 to 25.

PUNCH QUIZ QUESTION 1

What do you do with a "jigger"?

A) Dance

B) Open Bottles

C) Shake Drinks

D) Measure Drinks

STIRRUP CUP

1 PINT LIGHT RUM	3 Oz. Lime Juice
1 1/2 Oz. Brown Sugar,	6 Oz. Pineapple Juice
Dissolved in Water	

Serve in punch bowl with ice. Provide highball glasses filled with cracked ice and decorated lemon peel spiral.

Serves 8.

FRUIT RUM PUNCH

1 1/2 QTS. LIGHT RUM
6 Oz. Pineapple Juice
10 Oz. Orange Juice

10 Oz. Lemon Juice
1 1/2 Lg. Bottles of Ginger Ale

Pour into a container and let steep for 1 hour.

Add ginger ale or soda. Pour over block of ice in a punch bowl and stir. Decorate with one pint strawberries, lemon and lime slices.

Serves about 30.

HOT-BLOODED MARY

1 QT. VODKA
1 Qt. Tomato Juice
2" Stick Cinnamon

1/8 Tsp. Cloves
1 Tbsp. Worcestershire Sauce

Combine tomato juice, cinnamon, cloves, Worcestershire Sauce. Cook over low heat about 15 minutes. Add salt and pepper to taste.

Add lemon juice and pour in vodka just before serving.

Use Old Fashioned glasses or demitasse cups.

Serves 15.

MOM'S MILK PUNCH

Place **1 QUART WHISKEY**, 3 quarts milk and 4 ounces powdered sugar in punch bowl.

Beat well.

Strain into mug or glass and sprinkle with nutmeg.

Serves 14.

VODKA BOMBAY PUNCH

1 QT. VODKA	1/2 PINT ORANGE LIQUEUR
1 QT. SHERRY	2 QTS. Chilled Soda
1/4 Pint Maraschino Cherries	

Combine in a mixing bowl, without ice.

Set punch bowl in bed of crushed ice. Fill with punch and decorate with fruits. Add 4 quarts chilled champagne |ust before serving. Serve In punch cups.

Serves 15.

ICED FRUIT PUNCH

1 BOTTLE BRANDY	3/4 Cup Fresh Lemon Juice
1 1/2 Cup Freshly Squeezed	1 1/2 Cup Pineapple Juice
Orange Juice	1 (1 Liter) Bottle Club Soda

In large punch bowl, combine all ingredients. Add sugar to taste, if desired.

Add decorative ice ring or ice cubes. Garnish with sliced fresh fruit and mint leaves.

PUNCH QUIZ QUESTION 2

Which liquor can be set aflame?

A) Gin

B) Rum

C) Brandy

D) All of the Above

HEAVY ARTILLERY PUNCH

1 QT. WHISKEY
1/2 PINT GIN OR VODKA
1/2 PINT BRANDY
1 1/2 OZ. CLARISTINE
   BENEDICTINE

1 BOTTLE RED WINE
1 PINT RUM
1 Qt. Strong Tea
   or 1 Pint Orange Juice
1/2 Pint Lemon Juice

Combine ingredients in large punch bowl.

Add block of ice. Sugar syrup may be added for sweetening.

Decorate with twists of lemon peel.

Serve in punch cups.

Serves 25 to 30.

KNOCKOUT PUNCH

1 QT. WHISKEY
6 OZ. ORANGE LIQUEUR
Juice of 3 Lemons

Juice of 4 Oranges
1 Tbsp. Sugar

Mix ingredients. Pour over block of ice in punch bowl.

Add fruits as desired plus 1 quart chilled soda or iced tea.

Serve in punch cups.

Serves 12.

HOLIDAY PUNCH

1 1/2 QTS. GIN	1 1/2 Lg. Bottles of Chilled Soda
Juice of 8 Lemons	Water
4 Oz. Grenadine	

Combine juice, gin, and grenadine, pour over a large block of ice.

Add soda water.

Decorate with fruit.

Serves 12.

PUNCH QUIZ QUESTION 3
What do you do with a "Muddler"?
A) Stir Drinks
B) Crack Ice
C) Shake Drinks
D) Wipe Spills

HAWAIIAN WHISKEY PUNCH

4 QTS. WHISKEY	26 Oz. Pineapple Juice
12 Oz. Lemon Juice	48 Oz. Orange Juice

Pour over large block of ice in punch bowl and add 4 quarts of ginger ale and sugar to taste.

Decorate with orange, lemon and pineapple slices.

Serves 90 4 oz. servings.

MOON GLOW PUNCH

Pour **2 QUARTS VODKA**, 2 quarts orange sherbet and 4 quarts orange juice over ice and stir.

Serves 60.

OLD FASHIONED PUNCH

Stir together **4 QTS. OF WHISKEY**, 1 quart lemon juice, 1 pint Curacao and 2 quarts club soda. Add 4 dashes bitters.

Place block of ice in bowl before serving.

Serves 55 .

PINK PASSION PUNCH

Mix 1 gallon orange juice, 4 cups lemon juice, 2 quarts soda, 3 cups grenadine and **2 QTS. VODKA** together well. Pour over ice.

Serves 90.

PUNCH QUIZ QUESTION 4
Who was the Roman God of Drinking?
A) Thor
B) Bacchus
C) Jupiter
D) Ralph

PLANTATION PUNCH

Mix **2 QTS. JAMAICAN RUM**, 2 1/2 Cups Grenadine, 16 ounces orange juice, 16 ounces lime juice and 8 ounces pineapple juice together in a punch bowl.

Add large piece of ice. Add slices of two oranges, maraschino cherries, quart of fresh cubed pineapple or other available fruit.

Serves 40.

PUNCH ROYAL

4 BOTTLES SPARKLING BURGUNDY
4 BOTTLES STILL BURGUNDY
2 QTS. BRANDY

6 Oranges, Peeled and Sliced
1 Pineapple, sliced thin
1/2 Cup Sugar
Juice of 4 Lemons

Mix brandy, still burgundy and fruit with sugar. Let stand in refrigerator 20 minutes.

When ready to serve, pour over block of ice in bowl and add sparkling burgundy.

Serves 60 to 65.

SAUTERNE PUNCH

2 GAL. SAUTERNE
2 Qts. Pineapple Juice
2 Qts. Soda Water

6 Orange Slices
6 Lemon Slices
1 Pint Whole Strawberries

Mix pineapple juice and chilled wine.

Before serving, add soda and pour over ice in punch bowl. Garnish with fruit and mint sprigs.

Serves 70.

SANGRIA PUNCH

1 BOTTLE BURGUNDY	1 Sliced Orange
2 Lg. Sliced Lemons	2 Oz. ORANGE LIQUEUR
2 Sliced Peaches	2 OZ. BRANDY

Add sugar to taste and club soda if desired.

Serves 6.

STRAWBERRY PUNCH

Mix in punch bowl **1 GALLON SAUTERNE**, 1 can frozen lemon juice, **1 CUP RUM, 2 CUPS BRANDY**, 1 package strawberries and 2 cans pineapple chucks.

Add block of ice.

Serves 45.

WHISKEY PUNCH

2 QTS. WHISKEY	1 Pint Strong Cold Tea
1 Cup Sugar	2 Lg. Bottles Club Soda
1 1/2 Cups Lemon Juice	

Dissolve sugar in the lemon juice in a punch bowl.

Add whiskey and tea. Mix well. Add a block of ice.

Just before serving, pour in chilled club soda and stir gently.

Decorate with sliced fruits.

Serves 45.

ZOMBIE PUNCH

2 QTS. JAMAICAN RUM
2 QTS. PUERTO RICAN
RUM
1 QT. SPICED RUM
1 QT. 151 PROOF RUM

2 QTS. ORANGE LIQUEUR
2 Quarts Lemon Juice
1 Quart Grenadine
12 OZ. LICORICE LIQUEUR

Mix ingredients thoroughly. Chill with large cake of ice in punch bowl, letting it stand an hour or two before serving.

PUNCH QUIZ QUESTION 5

The Slovak toast "Na Zdravie" means....

A) To Your Health

B) You Buy

C) God Bless You

D) Nice Driveway

ANNIVERSARY PUNCH

2 QTS. CHAMPAGNE
2 QTS. WHITE WINE
2 QTS. SPARKLING
BURGUNDY

1 Qt. Frozen Strawberries
3 Tsp. Grated Lime Peel
Juice of 2 Limes

Combine strawberries, juice of limes and lime peel in a sauce pan. Simmer for 10 minutes, strain and cool, then pour over block of ice in bowl. Add chilled wines just before serving. Garnish with lime slices.

Serves 40.

BRIDE'S BOWL

2 QTS. RUM
1 1/2 CUPS PEACH BRANDY
1 Cup Lemon Juice
1/2 Cup Sugar Syrup
2 QTS. Soda Water

1 1/2 Cups Pineapple Juice, Unsweetened
2 Cups fresh Diced Pineapple
1 Pint Sliced Strawberries

Place Ingredients in punch bowl with block of ice.

Add other ingredients.

Add soda before serving together with the strawberries.

Serves 25 to 40.

CHAMPAGNE PUNCH

8 OZ. BRANDY
8 OZ. ORANGE LIQUEUR
2 BOTTLES CHAMPAGNE
1/2 Cup Lemon Juice

1/2 Cup Water
1 Cup Sugar
3 Oz. Maraschino
1 Lg. Bottle Club Soda

In a punch bowl, dissolve sugar in water and lemon juice.

Add brandy, maraschino and orange liqueur.

Mix well. Add block of ice.

Just before serving pour in chilled club soda and champagne.

Stir gently and garnish with sliced fruits and berries.

Serves 25.

CHRISTMAS PUNCH

1 QT. RUM	1/2 Cup Lemon Juice
1 QT. WHISKEY	1 Qt. Cold Strong Tea
1 QT. BRANDY	2 Tbsp. Bitters
1/2 QT. HERBAL LIQUEUR	1 Sliced Pineapple
2 BOTTLES CHAMPAGNE	1 Qt. Orange Juice
1 1/2 Cups Sugar	

Dissolve sugar in fruit juice in a punch bowl.

Add all other ingredients except champagne. Mix well. Add block of ice. Just before serving, pour in chilled champagne. Stir gently.

Serves 60.

CLASSIC EGGNOG

Beat yolk and whites of 8 eggs separately. Add 1/2 pound sugar to whites; beat until stiff. Combine beaten yolks and whites and mix thoroughly.

Add **8 OZ. RUM** and **1 QT. WHISKEY OR BRANDY**. Beat mixture. Add 1 pint heavy cream, 1 quart milk. Mix. Chill well. Serve with a light sprinkling of nutmeg on top.

Serves 20.

PUNCH QUIZ QUESTION 6
What is an Ale-Passion?

A) A Thirst

B) A Hangover

C) A Cocktail

D) A Large Mug

FISH HOUSE PUNCH

2 QTS. DARK RUM   **2 QTS. Water**
1 QT. BRANDY   **1 Qt. Lemon Juice**
6 OZ. PEACH OR APRICOT   **3/4 Lb. Sugar**
   LIQUEUR

Dissolve sugar in the water and lemon juice in a punch bowl.

Pour in Rum, Brandy and Liqueur. Mix well.

Add large block of ice, allow to get good and cold.

Stir thoroughly before serving.

Serves 50.

JERSEY GIN PUNCH

2 QTS. DRY GIN   **6 Oz. Grenadine**
1 1/2 Cups Lemon Juice   **2 Lg. Bottles Club Soda**
2 Qts. Orange Juice

Pour first four ingredients into a punch bowl and mix well. Add block of ice. Just before serving, add chilled club soda; stir gently and decorate with fruit slices.

Serves 50.

PATIO PUNCH

Mix **1 750ML BOTTLE WHISKEY**, 16 ounces grapefruit juice, 8 ounces fresh lime juice and 1 (2) liter bottle of ginger ale together.

Add ice and serve from a punch bowl or pitchers.

HOT GLOGG

Using a large pot, heat together **1 BOTTLE PORT WINE, 1 BOTTLE BURGUNDY WINE** and **1 BOTTLE POLISH VODKA** with 1/4 pound of small seedless raisins. Boil several minutes.

Into this, dip cheesecloth bag containing stick of cinnamon and handful of cloves; leave bag in liquid about a minute.

Serve drink in Old Fashioned glass or coffee cup with 2 almonds and a few raisins in each serving. If an Old Fashioned glass is used, put in a teaspoon to prevent cracking.

Sugar to taste, if desired.

Serves 24.

ONE TWO PUNCH

In container, mix two 46 ounce cans fruit punch, one 6 ounce can frozen orange juice concentrate, undiluted, one 6 ounce can frozen lemonade or limeade concentrate, undiluted and **750ml. LIGHT RUM**. Chill 2 hours.

Pour punch over block of ice in punch bowl. Float mint, strawberries, orange, lemon and lime slices on top.

Serves 22.

CONFETTI PUNCH

In large container, mix one 6 ounce can frozen lemonade concentrate, one 6 ounce can frozen grapefruit juice concentrate, one 16 ounce can fruit cocktail, drained and **750ml. LIGHT RUM**.

Chill for 2 hours, stirring occasionally. To serve, pour over ice in punch bowl. Add 2 (1) liter bottles chilled club soda. Stir gently.

Serves 8.

PUNCH QUIZ QUESTION 7

The only sure cure for a hangover is....

A) Alcohol

B) Aspirin

C) Raw Eggs

D) Time

THOUSAND YEAR OLD MULLED WINE

1 750 ml BOTTLE RED WINE	6 to 8 Cloves
½ CUP BRANDY	1 Cinnamon Stick
2/3 Cups Sugar	Orange Zest from One Orange

Pour wine into nonreactive saucepan and place over low heat. Do not use an aluminum pan, since it can leave a metallic taste in the wine.

Using zester or paring knives, remove orange zest from orange. Do not use any of the white part of the skin, since it is bitter. Lightly pound the zest with the back of a knife or mallet to release the aromatic oils and add to wine.

Squeeze the juice of the orange into the wine mixture. Add remaining ingredients.

When the wine begins to steam, it is ready to serve. Shut off the heat, strain the wine and serve.

An inexpensive bottle of Merlot is suggested for this recipe. For large parties, the recipe can be doubled.

FYI - Mulled wine has been served for a thousand years.

GOODNIGHT PUNCH

2 CUPS TEQUILA　　　　　**1 Qt. Ginger Ale**
2 Qts. Cranberry Juice　　**1/4 Cup Fresh Lime Juice**
3 Cups Pineapple Grapefruit
**　Juice**

Chill all ingredients. Pour into punch bowl.

Add ice ring if desired.

Makes 4 1/2 quarts.

ANSWERS TO PUNCH QUIZ

1) D - Measure Shots

2) D - All of the Above

3) B - Crack Ice

4) B - Bacchus

5) A - To Your Health

6) B - A Hangover

7) D - Time

INDEX

Answers to quiz questions are at end of chapters.

C

Devilish Chicken Chests, 50
Dolores' Rapturous Rum Cake, 111
Double Chocolate Rum Cake, 104
Double Fruit Soup, 140
Duck Breasts in Lingonberries and
    Wine Sauce, 52

E

Easy-Does-it Mincemeat, 77
Ed's Beer Batter Chicken, 20
Eggs:
    Eggs in Lush Mushroom Sauce,
    35
    Eggs-citing Omelet Filling, 83
    Rodney's Rum Omelet, 95
Eggs in Lush Mushroom Sauce, 35
Eggs-citing Omelet Filling, 83
Escalope Escapade, 141
E-Z Sole & Shrimp, 57

F

Fancy-Free Fillet of Sole with
    Mushrooms, 53
Fee-Fi-Fo-Fum Rum Cake, 107
Fiesta Guacamole, 113
Fillet Of Veal In Kumquat And
    Vodka Sauce, 66
Fish: See Seafood
Fish House Punch, 185
Flambeed Cherries, 163
Flemish Flank Steak with Onion
    Mushroom Beer Sauce, 13
Fowl:
    Breast and Wine and Have a
    Good Time, 44
    Bubba's Fried Chicken, 20
    Chef Conrad's Chicken Savoy,
    46

Fowl (continued):
    Chicken a la Lonny, 51
    Chicken a la Susie, 49
    Chicken En Civet, 47
    Chicken Hula, 46
    Chicken in Wine & Rosemary, 48
    Chicken Roulettes Florentine, 48
    Chicken Tequila Sunrise, 114
    Cluck-Cluck Chili, 137
    Cornish Hens with Black
        Raspberry Sauce, 128
    Devilish Chicken Chests, 50
    Duck Breasts in Lingonberries
        and Wine Sauce, 52
    Ed's Beer Batter Chicken, 20
    Richard's Roast Turkey with
        Cranberry Sauce, 121
    Roast Chicken with Raspberry
        Sauce, 130
    Roast Duck with Raspberry
        Sauce, 129
    Savory Baked Chicken, 123
    Sharon's Chicken Parisienne, 50
    Ten Minute Chicken Paprikash
        with Noodles, 43
    Whiskey Cock-A-Doodle, 80
    Zelda's Zesty Chicken Wings, 114
Fruit:
    Baked Apples Deluxe, 164
    Cordial Cranberry Sauce, 121
    Flambeed Cherries, 163
    Fruit Salad with Peach Schnapps
        Dressing, 127
    In The Pink Salad, 87
    Killer Fruit Kabobs, 96
    Lip Smacking Apple Stuffing,
        136
    Poached Fresh Fruit, 158
    Raspberry Berry Bowl, 162

Fruit (continued):
    Royal Flambeed Strawberries, 142
    Vegas Ginger Melon, 99
    Vodka in Melons, 65
    Whiskey Fruit Salad, 77
Fruit Rum Punch, 175
Fruit Salad with Peach Schnapps Dressing, 127

G

Garlic Shrimp Marsala Over Linguine, 58
Gaston Avenue Trifle, 61
Gin Swizzle, 173
Golden Apple Tart, 158
Golden Rum Cake, 103
Goodenuff Potato Salad, 11
Goodnight Punch, 188
Grandmother's Secret Ingredient Apple Pie, 167
Green Peas with Mint, 138
Grilled Shrimp A L'Orange, 83
Grilled Sole with Herbs And Butter Sauce, 70

H

Happy Hamilton's Sour Cream Cake, 168
Happy Hazelnut Cake, 73
Harlequin Parfaits, 147
Hawaiian Whiskey Punch, 178
Heady Honeydew Dessert, 25
Heavy Artillery Punch, 177
Herring Tartare And Mushrooms in Brine, 69
High Time Ham Rolls, 140
Holiday Hooch Squares, 107

Holiday Punch, 178
Hot Glogg, 186
Hot-Blooded Mary, 175
Hungry Hungarian's Goulash, 42

I

Iced Fruit Punch, 176
In The Pink Salad, 87
Irish Cream Pie, 166
Island Punch, 174
Italian Rum Cake, 108

J

Jazzy Ginger Cookies, 106
Jersey Gin Punch, 185
Jewish Meatballs, 14

K

Killer Fruit Kabobs, 96
Knockout Punch, 177

L

Lancer Meat Loaf, 37
Lazy Beef Casserole, 42
Let's Go Nuts Pie, 154
Lip Smacking Apple Stuffing, 136
Liqueurs: Pages 145 - 170
    Also see Cordials
Lola's Poached Salmon In Wine, 54
Lox Style Whitefish with Beet and Vodka Sauce, 67
Luscious Orange Vinaigrette, 139

M

Magnificent Melba Sauce, 161
Margo's Cheesy Beer Dip, 3
Marinades:
    Marvelous Marinade for
        Chicken, 97
    Mint Marinade for Lamb, 137
Marinated Swordfish, 23
Marvelous Marinade for Chicken,
    97
Max's Macadamia Nut Pie, 147
Midnight Punch, 173
Milk Chocolate Dessert Sauce,
    160
Mint Marinade for Lamb, 137
Mom's Milk Punch, 175
Moon Glow Punch, 179
Mushroom Lovers' Pronto
    Spaghetti Sauce, 60
Mystic Mousse, 162

N

New York Pork Terrine, 66
No-Peek Beef Casserole, 40
North Pole Whiskey Cake, 84
Norwegian Rum Cream, 109
Nuts To You Cheese Bars, 154

O

Oh My Gosh Ganache, 169
Old Fashioned Punch, 179
One Two Punch, 186
Onion Soup with Bourbon, 88
Orange Anisette Bundt Cake, 87

P

Passionate Potato Pancakes, 10
Patio Punch, 185
Paul's Pork Skewers, 16
PDQ BBQ Sauce, 95
Peach Almond Crunch Cake, 159
Peach Schnapps Preserves, 126
Peach Schnapps Scones, 126
Peachy Pork Loin, 124
Pecan Butterscotch Butter, 134
Peppermint Pie, 160
Peppy Pina Colada Dressing, 97
Pies:
    Angel Chocolate Pie, 152
    Apricot Cheese Pie, 157
    Butterscotch Banana Pie, 157
    Daiquiri Pie, 101
    Grandmother's Secret Ingredient
        Apple Pie, 167
    Irish Cream Pie, 166
    Let's Go Nuts Pie, 154
    Max's Macadamia Nut Pie, 147
    Peppermint Pie, 160
Pike in Vodka Tomato Sauce, 68
Pineapple Butterscotch Glaze and
Sauce for Ham, 132
Pineapple Punch, 173
Pink Passion Punch, 179
Plantation Punch, 180
Poached Fresh Fruit, 158
Pork:
    Anything Goes Jambalaya, 24
    Baked Ham with Peach Glaze,
        125
    Barnie's Pork Roast, 15
    Beer and Pork Chop Casserole,
        16
    Beer Barbequed Sausage, 18
    High Time Ham Rolls, 140

Pork (continued):
New York Pork Terrine, 66
Paul's Pork Skewers, 16
Peachy Pork Loin, 124
Pineapple Butterscotch Glaze
and Sauce for Ham, 132
Pork Cubes with Red Pepper
Dipping Sauce, 117
Six-Pack Sammy's Pork Ribs,
17
Succulent Sweet and Sour Pork
Chops, 123
Whiskey Ham Steak, 79
Pork Cubes with Red Pepper
Dipping Sauce, 117
Princeton Rarebit, 3
Punch Royal, 180
Punches: Pages 171 - 189

Q

Quick Swiss Fondue, 3

R

Randy's Rum Nuts, 111
Rarebit:
Princeton Rarebit, 3
Welsh Rarebit, 4
Raspberry Berry Bowl, 162
Raspberry Vinaigrette Salad
Dressing, 129
Real Boss Barbecue Sauce, 78
Richard's Roast Turkey with
Cranberry Sauce, 121
Roast Chicken with Raspberry
Sauce, 130
Roast Duck with Raspberry Sauce,
129
Rodney's Rum Omelet, 95

Royal Flambeed Strawberries, 142
Rum: Pages 93 - 111
Rum Lover's Brownies, 109
Rummy Raisin Ice Cream, 98
Rump Roast Repast, 13

S

Salad Dressings:
Black Raspberry Vinegar, 127
Blue Cheese and Beer Salad
Dressing, 7
Luscious Orange Vinaigrette, 139
Peppy Pina Colada Dressing, 97
Raspberry Vinaigrette Salad
Dressing, 129
Salmon River Steak Surprise, 55
San Antonio Tacos, 24
Sangria Punch, 181
Sassy Shrimp L'Orange, 139
Satiny Strawberry Mousse, 102
Sauces:
Buttery Barbeque Sauce, 134
Mushroom Lovers' Pronto
Spaghetti Sauce, 60
PDQ BBQ Sauce, 95
Real Boss Barbecue Sauce, 78
Saucy Steak Sauce, 14
Yummy Yogurt Sauce for Fruit,
134
Saucy Steak Sauce, 14
Sauterne Punch, 180
Savory Baked Chicken, 123
Schnorrer's Whiskey Schnitzel, 76
Scones:
Butterscotch Praline Scones, 133
Peach Schnapps Scones, 126
Seafood:
Al's Vodka Fish Dish, 68
Anything Goes Jambalaya, 24

197